I0426547

**Last of the Pioneers:
Or Old Times in East Tenn.;
Being the Life and Reminiscences of Pharaoh Jackson
Chesney
(Aged 120 Years)**

J.C. Webster

Last of the Pioneers
OR
Old Times in East Tenn.
BEING THE
Life and Reminiscences Of
Pharaoh Jackson Chesney
(Aged 120 Years)

BY

J. C. WEBSTER

KNOXVILLE, TENN.
1902

S.B. NEWMAN & CO.
PRINTERS & BOOK BINDERS.

CONTENTS.

SPECIAL ACKNOWLEDGMENT.

The writer is under special obligation to Mr. Robert Brice for valuable assistance in the publication of this volume. He has been a friend of the enterprise from its inception; and his aid and encouragement have made it possible for the public to have this work.

Mr. Brice is a prosperous, progressive farmer; an enterprising, public-spirited citizen; and, at present, a candidate for Register of Deeds for Knox County. He would honor any position of trust or responsibility to which his fellow citizens might call him.

Entered, according to Act of Congress, in the year 1902, by J. C. WEBSTER.

In the Office of the Librarian of Congress, at Washington.

LAST OF THE PIONEERS--PHARAOH CHESNEY

LAST OF THE PIONEERS--PHARAOH CHESNEY

PREFACE.

Dwelling alone, in a cabin of the most primitive description, on the summit of Copper ridge, five miles south of Maynardville, Union county, Tennessee, is unquestionably, one of the most remarkable men in the state of Tennessee, if not in the entire United States. He is remarkable not only on account of the great age to which he has attained, but equally so on account of the wonderful preservation of his bodily and mental powers. While it is impossible to assign the number of his years with absolute certainty, yet we are fully warranted in the assertion that he has undoubtedly passed the one hundred and twentieth mile-stone in his journey of life; and from collateral circumstances, we may infer that he may have reached, or even exceeded, a century and a quarter. The following pages will afford the reader some idea of his mental powers, nearly all of which were narrated by this old man within the present year (1902); and at this great age, he cuts and splits his wood, makes his fires, and does the principal part of his cooking. Besides, he not infrequently walks a distance of three or four miles and returns within a few hours. He has walked from his cabin to Cedar Ford, a distance of three miles, the voting place of his district, and cast his ballot for every republican candidate for president, from Lincoln to McKinley. He, himself, is at a loss for the cause of his remarkable vitality; as he has been by no means a teetotaler, or strictly temperate in his habits. He laughingly remarks that many of the modern laws of health would have to be reversed in his case. He has been sick only a few times in his life. While it has been his good fortune, under the peculiar regéme of his two masters, to escape much of the drudgery usually falling to the lot of a slave, he has been, nevertheless, a very industrious man, active and energetic. He was fond of most of the old-time sports, and his great strength and activity caused his recognition in games and feats of strength.

Not less wonderful than his physical powers have been the strength and accuracy of his memory. In this respect, he is truly a prodigy. The incidents and occurrences of his past long life are apparently as vivid and clear to his mind as though removed but

9

a few months in time. This fact induces the reflection that had he been reared under unfettered social conditions, and accorded the advantages of an education commensurate with the capacity of such a giant intellect, and with all the resulting powers of a liberal culture, he would easily have been the peer of B. K. Bruce, Fred Douglass, or Booker Washington. Let us fervently hope that history may never so far repeat itself that there may prevail a social condition or institution, that may prove a barrier to the progress of the human race; to quench the light of a glorious mind in the darkness of ignorance; or to prevent a human soul from achieving the destiny intended for it by the Creator.

THE HOME OF PHARAOH CHESNEY

INTRODUCTION.

About the time the pioneers of Tennessee were having their mightiest struggles in the effort to establish the first republic west of the Alleghanies; about the time that John Sevier was making the supreme effort of his life in behalf of the state of Franklin; and about the time that John Tipton and his followers were making an equally heroic struggle to maintain in the colonies the government of North Carolina, there was born, on the banks of the picturesque Roanoke, at the little village of Clarksville, in Mecklenburg county, Virginia, a yellow lad, who was destined to witness, through a part of three centuries, the process of change and development, at the hands of man, of a wilderness, inhabited by wild and savage beasts, and scarcely less wild and savage men, into a country, blessed with every refinement and convenience of a progressive age. He was destined to live, witness, and realize the most sanguine hopes, and the full fruition of the labors and privations of these sturdy pioneers, who first led the way into the vast trackless wilderness, and bravely met the dangers, and with a fortitude hardly equaled in the experience of mankind, endured the countless hardships incident to the settlement of this fair country of ours. The name of this yellow lad was Pharaoh Jackson. Born within a half dozen years of the signing of the Declaration of Independence, and still remarkably vigorous in mind and body, at the end of the first year of the twentieth century, he has observed the clearing of the forest, the subduing of the savage, the erection of the log-cabin school and church house, the establishment of the simplest forms of government to meet the necessities and requirements of a band of settlers, and all the rude and primitive practices of a helpless and dependent people. Later on he has seen the experiment of more elaborate forms of government made, until, in the fullness of time, he has seen established in our country, one of the best governments on earth, creating and fostering the most benign and glorious institutions ever vouchsafed to a deserving people. He has been a witness to the fact that this noble heritage has not been without the most serious cost to the noble men and women who have bequeathed it to us. Many of our most cherished privileges are the dear purchase of the blood of our fathers. The civil and religious liberties that no one ever thinks of denying to us, and our entire immunities from the dangers of a lurking, savage and treacherous foe, are greatly in contrast with times and conditions within the life and memory of Pharaoh Jackson. Apparently to him as yesterday, it was more the rule than the exception to be rudely awakened from a sweet slumber by the savage howlings of hungry, ferocious wolves, or the blood-curdling war-whoop of the savage Indian. Then scarcely a road deserving the name was to be found within the present state of Tennessee. He has lived to see macadamized turnpikes putting the teamster within easy reach of every center of trade. Then, the only vehicle of travel was the rude, rumbling, rough, home-made wagon. He has lived to see, in all their beauty, convenience, and perfection, our modern wagons, buggies and carriages. He has seen railroads spanning the continent, carrying civilization, art and improvement to the far west. He saw the Indian gliding along the rivers of Old Virginia in his birch-bark canoe, and he saw the first steamboat that ever ascended the Roanoke river. He has picked cotton from the seed many a day, and about a pound of the fiber was the result of his labor, and he has lived to see a machine that would separate a thousand pounds of cotton from the seed in a day. He has lived in a time when it took two days for a letter to go from New York to Philadelphia, now he sees mail delivered to every family, six days in the week. Then the postage on a letter was 40 cents, now it is only 2 cents.

He was a young man when the government was established at Washington, and when the young republic made its first effort at territorial expansion in the acquisition of Louisiana, he was scarcely twenty-five.

He was about twenty when Whitney invented the cotton gin, and remembers the slaves talking of the "Yankee machine" that would do the work of a thousand negroes. When he was about ten years old, a cluster of log huts which had been built in the Ohio valley, was called Cincinnati, and this same pioneer settlement has, during his lifetime, become the metropolis of the great state of Ohio, with a water front of ten miles.

Suppose, for instance, that when he was fifty years of age, his master had taken him to Fort Dearborn, on Lake Michigan. He would have found a little settlement of about a dozen log cabins, which the settlers had named Chicago, (1833). If he had lived there until the present time he would have seen this little mud village become the fourth largest city in the world, with over three and a half millions inhabitants, the greatest railroad center, and the greatest grain and meat market in the world.

Or, suppose he had been born in New York City. When about ten years of age, he would have witnessed the inauguration of Washington, as the first president of the United States (1789). When twenty, he could have witnessed the laying of the corner-stone of the City Hall (1803). At about twenty-two, he could have seen the first free school incorporated in the city (1805). When he was twenty-five, he could have seen Robert Fulton make the trial trip of the Clermont, the first effort at steam navigation in America (1807). In the same year he might have assisted, in some way, in surveying, and officially laying out the city. He might have crossed over to Jersey City when the first steam ferry was established, when about thirty years of age (1812). At the age of forty, he might have joined in the demonstrations in honor of General Lafayette's visit, when he was given the freedom of the city (1824). He might, the next year, have seen lighted the first gas lights used in the city (1825). In the same year, he might have participated in the imposing ceremonies attending the formal opening of the Erie canal, when Governor Dewitt Clinton wedded Lake Erie and the Atlantic ocean by pouring a keg of the lake water into the ocean (1825). He would have been fifty-four when the terrible scourge of Asiatic cholera visited the city; and three years older when the terrible conflagration of 1835, lasting three days, destroying 600 houses and $20,000,000 worth of property.

Had he gone to St. Louis when he was thirty-five years old, he could have assisted in erecting the first brick building in the city (1813). When about forty, he could have seen the first bank established (1816). Next year (1817), he could have witnessed the arrival of the first steamboat.

When he was forty-six the city would have received its first charter (1822). He would have witnessed the great prosperity of the city attended by many adversities. In 1785 and 1844 by great floods, occasioned by the swelling of the "Father of Waters;" in 1837 and 1847 by financial distress; in 1832 and 1848 by cholera; and in 1849 by fire.

Baltimore was well started as a town when Pharaoh Jackson was born, but he was nearly eighteen years old when it was made a city and a mayor chosen (1796).

Thus, it may be seen from the mention of these contemporaneous events that the subject of our sketch is older than most of the distinctive features, and the conveniences that belong to the great metropolitan cities in the United States; and, that had he lived in any of these great cities, he would have witnessed the first use of all the great inventions and improvements that have been perfected within the century just completed.

Not only has he been a living witness to the marvelous inventive and constructive genius of the nineteenth century, and the gradual displacement of the primitive methods and customs, by those more modern and effective, but he has also witnessed the introduction of some of the greatest household and economic inventions.

During his life-time have occurred some of most notable events of history. We shall mention only a few, with the remark that the occurrence of these events reached his ears as matters of news, and that at the present writing he remembers with distinctness, the impressions made upon his mind, and describes them with historical accuracy, dates excepted. Adoption of the Constitution (1787), Whitney's cotton gin (1793), Purchase of Louisiana (1802), Duel, in which Aaron Burr killed Alexander Hamilton (1804), Burr's memorable trial at Richmond, before Chief Justice Marshall, for treason (May, 1807), Fulton's steamboat (1807), War of 1812, the Seminole War (1835), as well as all the leading events of more recent times.

14

While he was yet a young man, assisting his master's other slaves in clearing out the canes in the bottoms of the "Roanoke and Dan," Virginia and all the states south except South Carolina, extended to the Mississippi river. North Carolina included the present state of Tennessee, Virginia included the present state of Kentucky and West Virginia, and Florida belonged to Spain. He has lived to see Ohio, Indiana, Illinois, Michigan, Wisconsin, and Minnesota carved out of the Northwest Territory--as well as the purchase, settlement, and development of all the great empire west of the Mississippi, and has joined in celebrating the addition of thirty-three new stars to the original thirteen on the American flag. He has not only lived to see the formation of this vast republic of ours by the voluntary union of so many independent states, but he witnessed the sanguinary struggle in which the fairest land under the sun was drenched in blood as a result of the dismemberment of this union. He has seen the boys in blue marching under the stars and stripes, and the boys in gray marching under the stars and bars, each fighting for a principle regarded as sacred and precious as life. And after this bloody civil strife, he has seen the white-winged angel of peace hover over this heaven-favored land, and later, when a foreign foe disputed the cherished rights of Americans, has seen these battle-scarred veterans, marching under the same flag, actuated by the same motives, and fighting for a common cause.

But the triumphs of war have been no less great and remarkable than have those of peace. Inventive and constructive genius in the palmy, quiet days of peace, have made conquests of far greater consequences to mankind than have been the victories gained on fields of battle. The little narrow creek meadow cut with an old Dutch scythe when Pharaoh Jackson was a full grown man, has been lengthened and widened until it has grown from one acre to fifty on account of the invention of the mowing machine. Instead of the reap-hook to cut the grain, and a wooden flail to beat it out of the straw, the great wheat ranches of the west have machines to cut, thresh, clean, and sack the grain. Equally great changes, improvements and revolutions have taken place in every branch of human industry. Since the boyhood of

15

our sketch, great and mighty changes have swept the face of our great country. Progress in the arts and sciences has brought about so many and such varied improvements, and has occasioned such diversified industries in order to keep pace with human needs and ambitions, that in the space of this remarkable life-time, the face of nature has undergone a transformation as sweeping and wonderful as that of the reputed wizard with his magic wand.

The miserable wigwam of the savage Indian gave way to the unpretentious but comfortable hut of the settler. This, in turn, as ambition prompted and prosperity permitted, was transformed into the old colonial mansion, the only evidence of which, enduring to the present, is a heap of stones, and fragments of decayed timbers, scored in a primitive forest a hundred years ago. Beside these ruins, rendered sacred by time, tradition, and association, stands today the stately mansion, the acme of architectural design and mechanical execution.

The forest, no longer affording a refuge and shelter for the skulking savage lying in wait for his pale face brother, or the natural home of the bear, the deer, or the turkey--the hunter's paradise--has been leveled by the woodman's axe, and has become the fertile field, teeming with plentiful harvests of golden grain, or carpeted with luxuriant herbage where flocks and herds roam at will. The splashing water-fall, beside which, perhaps the tired hunter sat and rested, or perchance the Indian warrior seated by the side of its sparkling waters, and gazing into its clear, limpid depths, wooed his dusky mate, is directed by the hand of the artisan in an artificial channel, and made to turn the wheels of such machinery as contribute to the wants of an ambitious and a progressive people. The howl of the wolf, the scream of the panther, or the war-whoop of the savage no longer echo upon our hillsides or in our valleys. Such sounds were once the common but unpleasant music that greeted the ears of our forefathers. Old Uncle Pharaoh has heard all that in his time, and has been permitted to live to see a time when humanity may, after the day's toil, retire in peace and security, and in sweet repose, await the coming of the dawn. The summons for him to answer the roll-call on the other shore has been delayed until the mighty struggles for independence are over, and all the garments once dyed in blood have changed to mantles of ministering charity, and the white-winged angel of peace has hovered over our country. Like good old Simeon, he is ready, and exclaims, "Lord, let thy servant depart in peace; for mine eyes have seen thy salvation."

But the point sought to be made by these observations and illustrations, is that our country has not only passed through all these changes, but has done so within the space of a human life. This life, prolonged to a remarkable length, through the mercy and wisdom of Him "who doeth all things well," is perhaps the most wonderful survival of three centuries. This life has witnessed the beginning of what has culminated through the genius of man, aided by the forces of nature, in achievements that are today the wonders of the age. His eyes have followed each step from the uncertain experiment through each round of improvement in the ladder of perfection, until the topmost round is reached; and as genius pauses and surveys below him the century's conquest, and just as he shades his eyes in the effort to penetrate the invisible realms of the spirit world, a voice echoes, "Thus far and no farther."

But the mighty pendulum of time has not yet reached the limit of its ever-widening arc; time is yet swinging around the mighty circle of the ages; history must go on repeating itself; the lost arts must be restored to the world; and the changes to come will be more momentous than those of the past. Following in the track of the mighty march of time, nations and people yet unborn will view with silent wonder wrecks of today's greatness outgrown and superseded by achievements yet to be.

INSTANCES OF GREAT LONGEVITY.

The feature of this work which will no doubt carry with it the greatest weight of interest is the fact of the great longevity of the principal narrator. And while such instances are rare and isolated, yet history abounds in many examples of persons who have attained to a remarkable old age. A table was prepared by

Mr. Easton, of Salisbury, England, giving some of the most noted names on record, of Europeans and Asiatics.

	Date	Aged
Appollonius of Tyana	99	130
St. Patrick	491	122
Attilia	500	124
Leywarch Hêw	500	150
St. Coemgene	618	120
Piastus, King of Poland	861	120
Thomas Parr	1635	152
Henry Jenkins	1670	169
Countess of Desmond	1612	145
Thomas Damme	1648	154
Peter Torton	1724	185
Margaret Patters	1739	137
John Rovin and wife	1741	172 & 164
St. Mougah or Kentigern	1781	185

Facts prove that, in circumstances favorable to extreme longevity, the Europeans, the most polished communities, have no pre-eminence over the tribes of Africa, the least advanced in the social scale. Doctor Pritchard, from various sources, collected a variety of remarkable instances of negro longevity, of which the two following are samples:

December 5, 1830, died at St. Andrews, Jamaica, the property of Sir Edward Hyde East, Robert Lynch, a negro slave in comfortable circumstances, who perfectly recollected the great earthquake of 1692, and further recollected the person and equipages of the lieutenant-governor, Sir Henry Morgan, whose third and last governorship commenced in 1680, viz., one hundred and fifty years before. Allowing for this early recollection the age of ten years, this negro must have died at the age of one hundred and sixty years.

*Sear's Wonders of the World, pp. 31-32.

Died, February 17, 1823, in the bay of St. Johns, Antigua, a black woman named Statira. She was a slave, and was hired as a day laborer during the building of the jail, and was present at the laying of the corner-stone, which ceremony took place one hundred and sixteen years ago (1823). She also stated that she was a young woman grown when President Sharp assumed the administration of the island which was in 1706. Allowing her to be fourteen years old at that time, we must conclude her age to have been upwards of one hundred and thirty years.

*Sear's Wonders of the World, pp. 31-32.

The same historical source from which the above instances were derived, furnish many more similar examples. These facts and illustrations are sufficient to show that there is no physical law forbidding the negro from attaining a longevity equal to that of the European in circumstances friendly to it; while placing the European in subjection to the same amount of toil in the West Indies, or planting him amid the swamps, the luxuriant vegetation, the inundation, and heat of Western Africa, and his term of life would not, in general, come up to the negro standard.

It was a well known fact among the early settlers that some of the Indians attained to a very old age, and were represented by members of their tribe to be much over one hundred years.

Humboldt, speaking of the native Americans, says, "It is by no means uncommon to see at Mexico, in the temperate zone, half way up the Cordillera, natives, and especially women, reach a hundred years of age. This old age is generally comfortable; for the Mexican and Peruvian Indians preserve their strength to the last. While I was at Lima, the Indian, Hilario Sari, died at the village of Chiguata, four leagues distant from the town of

Arequipa, at the age of one hundred and forty-three. She had been united in marriage for ninety years to an Indian by the name of Andrea Alea Zar, who attained to the age of one hundred and seventeen. This old Peruvian went, at the age of one hundred and thirty years, a distance of from three to four leagues daily on foot."

A REMARKABLE NEGRESS.

The Pennsylvania Inquirer, of July 15, 1835, contained this notice: Curiosity--The citizens of Philadelphia and its vicinity have an opportunity of witnessing at the Masonic Hall, one of the greatest natural curiosities ever witnessed, viz.: Joice Heth, a negress, aged, one hundred and sixty-one years, who formerly belonged to the father of George Washington. She has been a member of the Baptist church for one hundred and sixteen years, and can rehearse many hymns, and sing them according to former custom. She was born near the old Potomac river, in Virginia, and has, for ninety or one hundred years, lived in Paris, Kentucky, with the Bowling family.

All who have seen this extraordinary woman are satisfied of the truth of the account of her age. The evidence of the Bowling family, which is respectable, is strong, but the original bill of sale of Augustine Washington, in his own hand-writing, and other evidences, which the proprietor has in his possession, will satisfy even the most incredulous.

A lady will attend at the hall during the afternoon and evening for the accommodation of those ladies who may call."

A Mr. Lindsay was then exhibiting this aged negress at Philadelphia. Mr. Barnum, the great showman, was then on the lookout for some great curiosity, and went to Philadelphia to endeavor to purchase this novel exhibition. The first price put on the old woman was three thousand dollars, which Barnum declined to pay. He offered one thousand, which was finally accepted, and he exhibited her to immense throngs of people in all the large cities of the United States, until the following February, when old Joice Heth died, literally of old age.

The best description of this old negress is given by Mr. Barnum himself. "Joice Heth was certainly a remarkable curiosity, and she looked as if she might have been far older than her age as advertised. She was apparently in good health and spirits, but from age or disease, or both, she was unable to change her position; she could move one arm at will, but her lower limbs could not be straightened; her left arm lay across her breast, and she could not remove it; the fingers of her left hand were drawn down so as to nearly close it, and were fixed; the nails on that hand were nearly four inches long, and extended above her wrist; the nails on her large toes had grown to the thickness of nearly a quarter of an inch; her head was covered with a thick bush of grey hair; but she was toothless and totally blind, and her eyes had sunk so deeply in their sockets as to have disappeared altogether.

Nevertheless, she was pert and sociable, and would talk as long as people would converse with her. She was quite garrulous about her protege "dear little George," at whose birth she declared she was present, having been at the time a slave of Elizabeth Atwood, a half sister of Augustine Washington, father of George Washington. As a nurse, she put the first clothes on the infant, and she claimed to have "raised him." She professed to be a member of the Baptist church, talking much in her way on religious subjects, and she sang a variety of ancient hymns. In proof of her extra-ordinary age and pretensions, Mr. Lindsay exhibited a bill of sale, dated February 5, 1727, from Augustine Washington, county of Westmoreland, Virginia, to Elizabeth Atwood, a half sister and neighbor of Augustine Washington, conveying 'one negro woman named Joice Heth, aged fifty-four years, for and in consideration of the sum of thirty-three pounds, lawful money of Virginia.' "

* Life of P. T. Barnum, pp. 57, 58.

SARAH JENIFER, OF WASHINGTON, D. C.

Apropos to the foregoing, we clip from the National *Tribune* of October 1, 1885, the following notice of an aged negress of that city:

"Remarkable instances of longevity are sometimes found among the colored people. Sarah Jenifer, who was known to be one hundred and twenty years old, died in this city last week. Her eyesight, and indeed most of her physical and mental faculties, showed slight impairment until within a year past. She reared nineteen children, many of whom were similarly prolific, and, as may be imagined, she left a family of grandchildren down to the fourth and fifth generations, numbered by hundreds. Three of her surviving children are past ninety."

CLARKSVILLE, HOME OF MY CHILDHOOD.

I was born and reared in the town of Clarksville, Mecklenburg county, in Old Virginia, and this is why I always speak of Clarksville as my childhood home. This beautiful town, built on a lovely strip of level bottom land, was at first laid out on the south side of the river, just below where the Roanoke and Dan come together. The river still goes on to the ocean under the name of the Roanoke, but we all got used to calling the name of both rivers. There was, from my earliest recollection, a considerable settlement on the other side of the river, called Klipper's Landing, but after the steamboats began making regular trips to the town and above, quite a town sprung up across the river; and so, we might say, that Clarksville is situated on both sides of the river. Old Master Jackson had a large plantation and a magnificent home just below town, but almost joining it. Old Master Johnathan Jackson did a great deal of business in town, while young master, Corbin Jackson, was a stock dealer, and often took me on his buying trips to assist him in bringing back the stock he would buy. It was on one of these long trips buying up droves of cattle and sheep, that he came down into Tennessee, as far down as Surgoinsville, Hawkins county, that he became so favorably impressed with East Tennessee, that he was determined to one day make his home somewhere along Clinch mountain, in the beautiful valley.

Speaking of Clarksville, I do not believe the Creator ever made a place more fit for a life of pleasure and happiness than this town and country. The land was everywhere rich; there was plenty of fine timber and good water; the forest abounded in all kinds of game, from a ground squirrel to a bear; and every stream was full of fish, that could be caught without difficulty. Almost every old settler lived on his own large plantation, in a fine mansion, owned a number of slaves, and had become rich during the few years since the settlement of the country. These settlers, most of whom were old men when I was a mere boy, had turned their attention toward the raising of such products as commanded a ready market, either at home or abroad. Boats were built at Clarksville and at many other points, which were loaded with all kinds of produce, and taken down through North Carolina to the ocean, where it was loaded on ships. Tobacco was one of the principal shipping crops, and many large plantations were devoted almost entirely to raising it. Back farther in the hills and mountains, there were not as large plantations and as fine mansions as were found in the valleys and along the rivers. There were not so many slaves, but what few there were seemed contented and happy. The people lived equally as well, and had plenty to sell. Every Saturday wagons would come in from the hills and mountains to Clarksville, bring in loads of fruit, fur skins, chickens, butter, eggs, maple sugar, feathers, pine tar, ginseng, and often deer and bear meat. These articles they produced in great abundance, and usually bore a fair price. It was sold to the stores or to the shippers, or exchanged for salt, thread, indigo, nails, powder, lead, and such manufactured articles as the merchants kept for sale. There was not much money in circulation, neither did the people need or want it. I sometimes yet wonder how and why the world ever took such a notion for money. I can remember when bartering was all the go, and everybody did it. A bushel of corn or potatoes, or five pounds of meat for a day's work. So many pounds of feathers, tobacco, maple sugar, or butter for a yard of cloth, etc. Everybody understood what the custom of the country was, and very few buyers or sellers would undertake to make a bargain that was different from the regular custom. I have watched this old custom gradually give way, and money to come into use, and my

24

opinion is that the old style of trading was simpler, more easily understood, and was much fairer to the seller than to have a money value attached to every article. Very few persons ever raised just enough of everything they wanted for their own use. Of some things they raised more, and of other things they produced less than they needed; and so this was remedied by an exchange of articles, this deal being called bartering.

I remember my first bartering. As I have told you, the streams abounded in fish, which were easily caught. The merchants kept salt-fish in the stores to sell, but some of their customers preferred fresh fish. So the merchants were glad to exchange the salt-fish for the fresh ones, and as this just suited me, I made many trades with them. The salt-fish would keep for any length of time, while the fresh ones had to be used at once.

In addition to this being a land of plenty to eat, and of peace and prosperity, there was, also, plenty of amusements of all kinds to keep up a fellow's spirits. No use of dying of the "blues" on a plantation of darkeys. These were generally allowed liberty to go where they pleased on the plantation, and, just so a man did a good day's work, and the feeding and wood-chopping besides, he was allowed to enjoy himself in any reasonable way, so no harm or damage was done. As for myself, I would have been content to spend all my days, as I once did, at my old childhood home. It was all the freedom my heart could ever wish, and if I had had my choice I would never have left there. But the saddest day in all my life came to me when I was told that my beloved wife and children must be taken one way, and that I must go another. A more cruel blow could not have been given to me. I could not have felt worse if I had been told that we were all to be killed. It seemed to almost break my poor wife's heart; and the sad thought has always been with me, whether the poor creature ever lived after our separation. Our four children were grown, and one of them married to a man by the name of Jones, who were both sold and taken to Lexington, Kentucky. Of the other three I have never seen nor heard of since we were separated. During the many years since all of us that were living became free. I have contemplated making a search--like a mother partridge for her scattered brood-- for them; but this life, though long, has been so full of all kinds of cares and duties that this supreme desire of my heart must go unsatisfied. My day of life, I fully realize, is too far spent, and the shades of its evening are closing too close around me to permit the faintest prospect of my ever again seeing the home of my childhood's happy days, which I learn is all changed, save in name and location; much less to ever behold, on the shores of time, the faces of my loved ones, so cruelly taken from me. But the solace of my declining days has been, that as my feeble, tottering frame approaches nearer and nearer to the silence of the grave, my faith grows stronger, and the way becomes brighter as visions of blissful immortality greet my disconsolate mind. I feel that I have now nothing to live for, and am simply waiting for my Master's call; and when that summons shall come, that same sustaining faith whispers to me, that perchance some of those loved ones have already gone on before me, and may be the first to greet me over there. That ever-abiding faith in my Creator's power and wisdom also assures me that though my bones are not buried at my old Virginia home--as my most cherished wish has been--that when the great roll-call of heaven is made, that here in Sunny Tennessee, my grave will be found by Him, and I shall awake and come forth and enter upon that new life, which shall know neither decay nor death, and where severed ties and dismembered families will enter upon a perpetual union, "Where the wicked cease from troubling and the weary be at rest."

THE FIRST STEAMBOAT ON THE ROANOKE AND DAN.

I remember as well as if it occurred but a month ago the occasion of the coming of the first steamboat up the Roanoke to Clarksville. We had all heard of steamboats, but there was not a half dozen people in all that country that had ever seen one, and but few, I think, had any correct idea of how one would look. I remember we darkies, after we heard that on a certain day a steamboat was coming to our town, would sit around and exchange ideas and notions as to how it would look. After seeing one we had many hearty laughs about how different it proved to be from what we imagined. For my part the strangest thing to me was how there could be enough iron about it and yet it not sink. About as silly was our wonder, when railroads were first talked of, how they could carry anything else after carrying enough sand to keep the wheels from slipping! One darkey being called upon for his opinion, said that the thing could not be; that no power in or on the boat could possibly move the boat; that it would be just like a man trying to lift himself over the fence by pulling up on his boot straps. About the funniest idea I heard given was by a numb-skull who said that the boat would have to stop running when the steam was used to whistle! But we all had to give it up, in spite of our logic, when the boat steamed into Clarksville.

The news had been circulated far and wide that a steamboat would come up to Clarksville from Weldon on a certain day. This was the occasion of a general holiday among all classes. Horses and mules were taken from the plow and hitched to all sorts of conveyances, and men, women and children came from all parts of the country, and collected on each side of the river. Seats were put up on the banks for the women and children; some of the men sat on their horses in order to see over the heads of the crowd, and many of the men and boys climbed into trees in order to be the first to see. Just below town the river makes a bend, and every eye was turned in that direction. Soon a shout went up from those in the trees saying that they saw the smoke and that she was coming. Then there was such a scramble as I have never seen since in order to get nearer the landing. Soon the black curling smoke could be seen by all, and in a moment more, the tall black smoke-stack loomed up just at the bend a short distance below us. Then the scramble for places was renewed, and shouts, and yells, and screams went up from the crowd lining each bank. As there was a large crowd on both sides of the river, there was much doubt and anxiety as to which the boat would land. The pilot, evidently considering ours as the largest crowd, began turning her prow toward our side, and just then the whistle began blowing, and the crowd on shore created such a scene as I have never before or since witnessed in my life. The shouts were deafening; women screamed and fainted, and children were frantic with the excitement. With mighty puffs and heaves, with the foam leaping and the waves dashing against the shore, the boat neared the bank. Two broad, thick planks were laid out upon which persons on the boat could come ashore. As soon as these had stepped on land, several of the crowd began crowding on the gang plank to go in and see the inside of the boat. About the time both planks were full the steam blew off with such force and noise that a regular panic ensued. In their fright several of those on the planks fell head long into the mud and water; again the women and children screamed, this time in fright; the small and weak in the crowd along the bank were run over, knocked down, and trampled upon in the wild, mad rush to get away from the escaping steam. Most of the crowd thought that the thing had exploded, and it was some time before the captain could restore order by the assurance that there was no harm. He took pains to explain all about how the safety-valve would let off the surplus steam, and prevent the boiler from bursting.

But I have not told you the worst. The horses had their nerves strung up to a high pitch already at the noise of the boat, and the tumult of the crowd. In their haste to get a position on the bank, many had alighted from their vehicles, and had left the horses unhitched. These, when the steam blew off, could stand it no longer, and broke away without driver, and went dashing and clattering pell-mell, helter-skelter in several directions, upsetting wagons and buggies, tearing down posts and fences, and pursued by dozens of yelping dogs, left the scene in the wildest confusion. Many people were run over and hurt, and several horses were crippled in the stampede. The crowd across the river, that had been disappointed in the boat's not landing on their side, now took in the situation, and set up the most tumultuous laughing, shouting, and clapping of hands that I ever heard. They enjoyed our discomfiture immensely.

After the panic was over, and order restored, speeches were made, wine and cider was passed around, and the captain spoke glowingly of the great advantages and possibilities of the steamboat, and what a great blessing it would prove to the world. If any one of that great crowd besides me is still living, he will join me in saying that that was the greatest day Clarksville ever had. Soon, this boat made regular trips to our town, and before we left that beloved place to come to Tennessee, other boats made regular trips up the Roanoke and Dan. They usually came steaming up after dark, beautifully lighted up, and the bands playing. Oh! we never grew tired of the glorious sight; it seemed to thrill us with new life. And though my ears are getting deaf, and my old eyes growing weak, I pine once again to hear the shrill steamboat whistle, and to see the beautiful lights and the streaming banners once more on the lovely river of my boyhood days. Truly, there is no time like the old time, and it will never come to us again.

[In spirit, if not in words, Uncle Pharaoh constantly reechoes the sentiment of the poet, in the following lines:]

"There are no days like the good old days,
The days when we were youthful;
When humankind were pure of mind,
And speech and deed were truthful;
Before a love for sordid gold
Became man's ruling passion,
And before each dame and maid became
Slaves to the tyrant's fashion."

THE INDIANS.

29

General Jackson used to say that the only good Indian was a dead Indian. He said that little Indians made big Indians, and that big Indians were always bad Indians; and in his battles with these savages, he told his soldiers to kill all of them, big and little. This made it pretty hard on the old squaws, but I know, from a long acquaintance with the Indians, that the women were generally as big liars and rogues as the men, and when they would be torturing a white person, that the women would often think of more cruel things to do than the men. Sometimes when a crowd of Indians would come to a settler's cabin to beg, the women would slip around the house and steal everything loose, while the men would keep the attention of the white people. You could never tell much about what an Indian was going to do. He might have come to kill you, and he would come up smiling in such a way as to make you believe he was the most friendly Indian in the world. An Indian could deceive a fellow about as well as some white folks can. I always knew that we colored people came from Africa, and that always satisfied me, but I always had a great desire to know where the Indians came from. I tried hard to find out all I could from the oldest Indians, but they had a great, long story about descending from some great, powerful tribe--something that had been told to them by the old men (tradition). But I never thought they knew anything certain about it themselves. They could not tell me anything about who made the mounds of earth to be found in many parts of Tennessee. We always called them Indian mounds, and supposed the Indians made them, but for what purpose, or when, they themselves seemed to know as little about it as we did. One thing only we do know--they were here when the white men first came, and that is all. Another thing, some of the Indians did not seem to know much about the flints or arrow-heads which can be picked up almost every-where. They could be picked up just the same when I was a boy in Old Virginia, and I never saw but a few Indians that could make them. The ones I saw them make were rough and ugly. They did not use the bow and arrow very much for they nearly all had guns, and had learned how to use them from the white people. But every Indian boy had to learn how to use the bow and arrow, and so well did they learn it that they seldom ever missed anything they ever shot at. Birds and animals which they shot were often not killed at once, but were so badly crippled by the rough flints on the arrows, that the Indians soon caught up with them and finished killing them. It was a funny sight to see them splashing in the creek after a wounded fish, bursting through the brush after a crippled turkey, or chasing through the woods after a wounded deer. But they were generally successful, and seldom failed to bring home the game.

But while the women were as bad as the men in some respects, in others they were very much better. They did not keep themselves much cleaner than the men, and neither gave themselves much concern on this score. But they were not half as lazy as were the men. In the chase or on the warpath the men were active and sprightly enough, but when about the lodge or wigwam, the lazy, good-for-nothing fellows would not do a lick of work in the way of preparing food or fuel, and all of the work now considered as belonging to men, was performed by the women. The animals brought in as game were skinned, cut up, and prepared into food by the women, and often the greedy hunters would turn in for dinner before it was half done, and devour all of it, before the women could get a share. The seed-corn had to be kept hidden from the men for when they would come in tired and hungry, they would eat up everything in sight. When the season came for planting, the women prepared the ground for the seed, planted the grain, and gave it such little cultivation as it ever received. The corn was most always planted in a rich, moist spot of ground, and did not require much work except to keep the weeds pulled out. They also planted beans, and raised abundant crops of them. They boiled beans and green corn together and made succotash which was very good. The Indians taught the white settlers how to raise corn. The Indians showed them how to deaden the timber by building fires at the roots of the trees, or by cutting a ring around the tree while the sap is flowing. They also showed them that where the land was not rich, if they would dig a hole and put into it a good sized fish, and then plant the corn in the hole with the fish, that they would always raise a big hill of corn, no difference how poor the land was. Speaking of corn I am sure that the Indians could never have existed without it. The land was rich, and it did not require much labor; when ripe it did not require to be gathered before winter, as it would stand all through the winter, and be sound in the spring. There was no other grain or vegetable that was so easily raised, that produced such great quantities, and took care of itself. The Indian might have subsisted on fruits, berries and game during the summer, but they really could never have lived and kept their horses alive through the winter without corn.

But raising the corn was not the hardest work that the Indian woman had to do. Whenever game became scarce in any locality, or the grass gave out, then the men would go to another place and decided on a location. When the time came to move the women had to carry all the luggage and the cooking utensils. The load one could carry was simply astonishing. The Indian men seemed to think it beneath the dignity of a hunter or a warrior to engage in any kind of manual labor.

But while the Indian was cruel, revengeful, deceptive, and indolent, still he had some redeeming traits of character. You have heard it said that he never forgave an enemy nor forgot a friend. Well, that was just about the case exactly. In all my dealings with these savage people, I have never observed much exception to that rule. For if you ever did one a kind act, he would never forget you, but we have often wished that they would sometimes forget. They would be very much like the old darkey was by his master. One day the old darkey's master gave him a chew of tobacco. The next day the old darkey come back and said, "Massa, don't one good turn deserve another?" Of course his master said "Yes." Then the old negro said, "You gave me a chew of tobacco yesterday, so that deserves another." So it was with the Indian. He would never forget you, and would always be coming back for something else; and if he didn't get what he wanted, he would conclude that you was not a friend to him, even though you had given him a dozen things. They would just hang around and beg and steal, or starve if you once began to give to them. So, many of the early settlers decided that it was best to let them be enemies and watch them than to feed and clothe them. For whenever you got on friendly terms with a lot of Indians, they would always be prowling around, day and night, and, as I said, if you denied them what they wanted, it would be sure to make them mad. They have been known to give up even hunting and fishing to live off a few settlers that wanted to keep friendly with them.

But if you had ever befriended one, especially if you had fed him well when he was very hungry, he would never forget your face, nor the favor, and if you ever got into trouble, he would do everything in his power for you, even at the risk of his life.

I once knew a hunter in Old Virginia, who went out one day in search of game. The whole country was a wilderness, and no roads, except here and there an Indian trail. He went so far out into the forest that he finally became lost, and when, at last, he decided to return home, he knew not what direction to take. He would occasionally cross an Indian trail but was afraid to follow it, fearing that he might come up with Indians who would, as he thought, most surely kill him. Or, one of the trails, if followed, would certainly lead him to one of their villages, where he would be captured and perhaps tortured. So, this man wandered about through the woods all day, with no thought of game, but only of reaching his cabin. Night finally came on, and weary and discouraged, he climbed up into a tree, taking his gun up with him. He climbed the tree in order to be out of the reach of bears or wolves that would soon be prowling around in search of food. He sat up in the tree and nodded, being so sleepy that he could scarcely hold on to the limbs. But about midnight his desire for sleep was taken away, when he heard, not far from the tree where he was, the solitary howl of a wolf. This was almost immediately answered by that of another, on the top of a ridge not far away. Soon the howls were coming from all directions. As they came nearer their blood-curdling yells almost chilled the blood in his veins. The moon was shining dimly, and by straining his eyes, he could see coming toward him a long, slim, dog-like animal. It came on up and began howling, jumping, scratching, and gnawing at the tree. In a few minutes other wolves were coming to the tree from all directions. Soon there must have been as many as fifty of these hungry creatures, howling, and gnawing at the tree. He is sure that they would have gnawed down the tree before morning, but as soon as they would begin to gnaw at the tree, they would begin to fight, which would be kept up for several minutes. Then, as soon as the fighting was over, they would come back to the tree. He sat in the tree and watched these savage brutes until daylight, when, one by one, they would look up at him and show their ugly teeth, and slink away. When the sun was fairly up they were all gone. But still he stayed in the tree until he was sure they had gone away a long distance, when he slid down from the tree, and started on, he knew not where. All day long, he wandered, tired and hungry, crossing logs and creeks, and climbing hills in hope of getting a glimpse of the settlement where his cabin was. He traveled on until it was nearly dark again, and he was so tired that he could scarcely walk and carry his gun. He was just thinking of looking out for a suitable tree in which to spend another night with the wolves, when he came to an Indian trail. He stopped in the trail to look each way (as a white man always did when crossing an Indian trail) and his heart almost sank within him at what he saw. Coming toward him, not a hundred yards away, was a band of about twenty Indians. When they saw him, they uttered a hideous yell, and made a rush for him. He stood perfectly still, and when they came up, they seized him, and handled him very roughly, and taking away his gun, pointed with angry and threatening gestures for him to move ahead in front of them. The trail led over hills and ridges for several miles to their village. They had just returned from a hunt, and had killed a deer, which they threw down to the women when they reached the huts, and each of the men immediately threw himself upon the ground and were soon asleep. Almost as soon as they arrived with the prisoner, they placed a guard of young men about him. They kept a very close watch over him all the while. After a little while, the deer was prepared, after their usual fashion, for being eaten, and the sleepers were aroused. They all went in a rush for the dinner, and none of them, except one, seemed to pay any attention to the captive. One of them came to where he was guarded and motioned for him to come. By the

34

time they had reached the food, the greedy hunters had taken all of it but one piece, which was large enough for two persons. This piece the Indian seized, and gave nearly all of it to the white man, keeping only a small piece for himself. This meat satisfied his hunger, and he was taken back, and the guard again placed round him as before. The Indians, now rested and refreshed, seemed to be consulting as to what should be the fate of the prisoner. All except the one who had given him the meat seemed to be in a very ugly humor, and he felt sure that it all meant no good for him, though he could not understand a word they were saying. Once in a while he could catch a word or two of broken English from the friendly Indian, which gave him hope that this Indian, having been with the white people long enough to learn some of their words, would have some friendly feeling for him, and would in some way prevent his being killed.

Soon dark came on, and the hunters who had captured him all went to sleep except one who would be left to guard him. One would only guard for a short time when another would be awakened, and this one would fall asleep. By and by, about midnight, it came the turn of the friendly Indian to guard, which he did until all the rest were sound asleep. Then the Indian arose very softly, and motioned for the white man to follow him. He did so, and after going a short distance from the camp, they came to a stump behind which was sitting the gun which had been taken from him, and upon the stump was a large piece of well-cooked meat. The Indian bade the white man take these, and then the Indian led the way by a different trail from that by which they had come. All the time after they left the stump, there was not a word said by either of them until they must have traveled several miles. Finally, the Indian stopped, and turning to the man said, "I have saved your life at the risk of losing my own. They had decided to put you to death, and if it should be found out that I have aided you in getting away, I would have a close call for my own life. I will no doubt be put to death in your place. But I came to your cabin a long time ago, hungry, tired, and pursued by my enemies who were seeking my life. If they had caught me, they would have killed me; but while I was in your cabin, and you were giving me food and shelter, they passed by, and you saved my life. Now I have saved yours. Keep this trail for a short distance further, and it will take you to the white settlements." So saying, the Indian turned quickly, and in a minute was speeding his way back to the Indian camp.

All the time the Indian was talking, the white man was trying to remember where he had seen the face that seemed to have something familiar about it. At last, he remembered that when the Cherokees and Chickasaws were making war on each other, that an Indian, that appeared to be in great distress and very much frightened, came to his cabin and begged for food and water. He would not stay outside to eat it, and while in the cabin a number of Indians passed by. He then recognized this friendly Indian as the one.

INDIAN TRADITIONS. UNCLE PHARAOH'S RECOLLECTIONS OF OLD TOKA.

Much of the Indian character, their modes of life, and warfare, their manners and customs, and many of their traditions, I learned from an old Chickasaw chief, named Toka, who resided at the Chickasaw Old Fields, near the Muscle Shoals, until his tribe was overpowered and driven out by the hostile Creeks and Cherokees. He then moved up nearer to the Cumberland settlements, and was one of the two Chickasaw guides employed by Col. James Robertson in his memorable Coldwater expedition against the Creeks occupying the old Chickasaw hunting grounds. Much of the success of this expedition was due to the knowledge of the country, and the fidelity of this old chief. It was he who informed Robertson and others of the Cumberland settlers that the Spanish traders were offering a regular bounty for the scalps of the white settlers, and were furnishing the Indians with guns and ammunition in consideration of their services in committing depredations on the whites. He still had the gun and blanket, and often spoke of the horse presented him as his share of the spoils, and in consideration of his services. Later, sad, dejected, and dispirited at the loss of their valued hunting grounds, and the dispersion of his tribe, he passed up the Tennessee river, his identity concealed, dwelling for a time, among the various tribes through which he passed, finally making his way to the extreme north-eastern part of the state, and becoming absorbed in name, with a tribe of Cherokees dwelling on the border line, secretly bewailing the fate of the nation of which he was once so proud to be a descendant. I was with him much, as he often came to Clarksville, and as always a great favorite with the whites. But I never knew what finally became of him.

He took great pleasure in relating the tradition as to the origin of the Chickasaws east of the Mississippi river. He said their ancient home was in Arkansas and to the westward; and, that when they decided to migrate across the Great Father of Waters, they took with them a pole, which was to serve them as a guide as to the direction they should taking each morning. When night came on, they encamped, and when halted for the purpose, they would set the pole upright in the ground, and next morning they would see which way it leaned, and would judge that the Great Spirit had caused it to point in the direction he designed them to take. They also took along a very large dog, that would serve them as a guard, by barking and warning them of the presence of their enemies. With their guard and guide, they journeyed on toward the great river; but before reaching it, they passed by a great sink-hole, and here was the last they ever saw of their dog. At night, they fancied they heard his piteous howls, and so long as the distance was not too great, when they took any scalps in their battles with their enemies, they would send them back and throw them into the sink-hole to the dog.

After crossing the Mississippi, they continued their journey until they reached the present site of Huntsville in Alabama. Here, they were in great doubt and uncertainty as to what direction to take, as the pole was in an unsettled condition for several days. This was considered as a bad omen, and many of the tribe passed on toward the east, into the Carolinas; but the others waited for the pole to become settled, which it did after a time, and pointed in a north-west direction. Each night the pole was planted, and each morning it pointed in the same direction, until they had crossed the Tennessee river, just above the Muscle Shoals. The first morning after crossing the river the pole stood perfectly upright, leaning in no direction. They waited for several days, but neither wind nor weather had the effect to change its position, and, as the country was all that their hearts could wish, they decided that this was truly the "promised land," and here they made their home until the culmination of their sad and melancholy fate at the hands of superior tribes, and the intrigues of their pale-face brother.

EARLY METHODS, MANNERS, AND CUSTOMS.

People who have grown up within the last thirty years can have but a very faint idea of the methods employed by our forefathers in nearly everything pertaining to domestic economy. Our grandmothers planted the cotton, gathered the fiber from the bowls when ripened, picked out the seeds by hand, carded the cotton with hand-cards into rolls, spun these rolls on a home-made spinning wheel into thread, colored this thread with home-made dyes, and wove it into cloth on a home-made loom. This cloth, coarse and strong, was cut out and made into garments of the most simple patterns, and worn with the same pride and satisfaction that the people now wear the ready-made fabrics with costly trimmings. No regard, whatever was paid to any dictates of fashion, and if some one wished to vary some old shape or form in a garment to suit themselves, they felt perfectly at liberty to do so, without any fear that they would become a laughing stock for being "out of style."

Woolen clothes, of course, were provided for winter wear, and the carding, spinning, and weaving were performed much in the same way as the cotton. Hemp shirts were frequently made for the slave boys and girls. These shirts could be cut, but not torn. Many a time, in crossing a fence, I have caught my shirt on a knot or splinter, and in jumping to the ground, have thrown my whole weight on my shirt, and have found myself hanging up against the fence, and my feet off the ground. Often in climbing saplings, I have hung myself on a knot by my tow shirt, but it never tore. The flax was prepared in a different way from the cotton and wool. The flax stalks were cut at a proper time and tied in bundles. These bundles were then placed in water so as to loosen the bark from the stalks. The bark was the part from which the thread was made. After the bark had become loosened, it was taken to a "break" which broke up the stems so that the bark, or fiber could be easily separated from the broken stems by drawing it repeatedly through the "hackle"--a board with a great number of sharp spikes driven through it. After other processes of preparation, it was ready to be spun into thread. But the spinning of flax thread required a different kind of wheel from the cotton or wool, and was called a "flax wheel." On account of the time and labor involved in the making of flax thread, not a great deal of it was made; but long after they ceased weaving the tow cloth, much thread was made for sewing leather, and for other purposes.

Much of the wool was used by being spun into yarn for knitting into stockings and gloves for the family. While the children would gather around the wide fire-place and pick cotton from the seeds; the mother or eldest daughter would be spinning thread; some one would be carding rolls; the father, apt as not, would be making a pair of shoes; a split basket, or "bottoming" a chair with splits. Sometimes the mother's "evening job" would be knitting, and when she would pay her neighbor a visit, she would invariably take her knitting along, and, during her stay, would frequently knit "the old man," as the husband was called, a pair of socks. But each member of the family, unless it was the baby, had some kind of work, and no one left the circle until one of the parents called out "bed-time." There were no lamps, and as a rule, the room was lighted by huge pine knots brought from a neighboring ridge. Often, however, home-made candles were used. These were made by pouring melted beef tallow into moulds in which a wick had been suspended. When these were cooled, the moulds were slightly heated, which loosened the candles. Mutton tallow was never used for this purpose, it being mixed with rosin and balm-of-gilead buds to form a very useful salve for cuts, sores, and burns.

The skins of the animals killed for meats, such as the cow and sheep, were tanned at home. The hides were soaked in a strong solution of lime and water, and the hair was removed. The surplus flesh still adhering to the hide, was then all scraped off, and finally the hide was soaked in a strong tan-ooze made from the bark of the chestnut oak, until experience taught the tanner that it was now fit for leather. Generally, each neighborhood contained a professional cobbler who went from house to house, and cut out and lasted the shoes for winter wear, as few used them in the summer season. After the shoe had been "lasted," that is, the eye-seams sewed, and fitted and pegged to the last, it required very little skill to peg on the bottoms and heels, which the farmer usually did himself on wet days. The last and pegs were home-made, and comfort and durability, and not beauty, were the prime considerations. In those days we never heard of corns on the toes--nature's penalty for pride. A pair of shoes were supposed to last a person for a whole year, and they were not put to any unnecessary use. It was a custom to go bare-footed--both men and women--to almost the church, when they would sit down and put them on. At a short distance from the church on returning home, they were taken off.

There was a great demand for the labor of every person who possessed the slightest mechanical genius. The man who could make split baskets, bottom chairs, make scrub brooms, and the various necessary household contrivances was considered a very useful person, and usually got plenty of work to do, and made a respectable living by doing such work. The baskets were carefully made of selected white oak splits, of different sizes and shapes, and for different purposes. The common farm basket was made strong, and in sizes to hold a peck, half-bushel, three pecks, and a bushel; and each readily sold for its fill of corn or wheat, or an equivalent in some other kind of produce. Other kinds of baskets were made for the housewife for holding her clothes, and household articles.

The chair seats were made of the best quality of hickory and white oak splits, and woven in fancy and difficult designs, and with ordinary use would last twenty years.

The chair maker was a man of more mechanical skill than the last referred to. He turned his posts out of good hickory, only partially seasoned. The rounds were of seasoned locust, turned with a shallow groove in the end that was driven into the post. The post then seasoning and shrinking down on these rounds, would render it impossible for them to ever become loose. Chairs made by "Uncle James Webster" in Knox county, over a half a century ago, are as strong and intact now as when first made by him.

The chair maker, having a turning lathe, and being usually a mechanic of sufficient skill, would generally also make the spinning wheels. These had to be made and balanced in the most accurate manner, or else they would be continually "throwing the band," which was most provoking to the spinster. The reel was considered the work of a great genius, and it is to be regretted that the inventor's name is lost in the dim and distant past. It consists of a very clever arrangement of interworking cog wheels, so that in turning the large wheel upon which is wound the thread, a sharp "click" indicates that a "cut" of thread has been wound. As services for spinning and weaving were charged for, as so much the "cut," it is difficult to see how the reel could have been dispensed with.

The main working parts of the loom could be made by almost any ordinary mechanic, but the "slays" were exceedingly tedious and difficult to make; and this gave rise to a new industry, and furnished employment to a "slay maker," who enjoyed quite a monopoly of his line, as he had few competitors. Old ones were continually giving out, and as these had to be mended, or replaced by new ones, he found plenty of work to do, and his services were in constant demand.

There was also the cooper whose trade was a very important one in the early settlements. He made the buckets, churns, lard stands, pails, barrels, and kegs. As these articles were in constant use, he was kept quite busy until the families were all supplied. The smaller vessels were made mostly of red cedar, and would last a life-time. The barrels and lard stands were made of good white oak, and were likewise very durable. Vessels made by these old-time coopers may be found at the present time, as sound and serviceable as they were half a century ago, but considered somewhat out of date.

But perhaps the most useful of all the mechanics in the early settlements was the blacksmith. His work covered a wider range of useful articles than any of the other mechanics. It is easy to see how in cases of emergency, the articles made by the other artisans mentioned, could have been substituted for; but it does not appear how a community could have existed without the services of a blacksmith. He made the plows, hoes, mattocks, wagons, and chains for the farmer; the augers, planes, nails, hammers, and chisels for the carpenter; the shovel, tongs, hooks, and andirons for the fireside; all the nails, hooks, staples, rings, bands, rods, and every kind of tool used by everybody. His iron came to him, not as it reaches the blacksmiths of today, in convenient sizes and shapes, as rods and band iron, but in large bars, several inches broad, and several inches thick, which had to be forged out and hammered down to the required sizes. These huge bars of iron were heated in a fire made of charcoal, burnt of pine or chestnut wood, often in a pit in the shop yard. While the blacksmith was burning his coal-pit, or using the light, sparkling fuel on his heavy bars of iron, the people of Virginia and Pennsylvania were bursting up, and building roads with the very things that revolutionized blacksmithing--stone coal-- and did not know its value. It is amusing to one who remembers the introduction of stone coal into the old-time blacksmith shop. There was almost as much prejudice evidenced by the people generally as by the blacksmith. Some said that it would burn and scorch the iron so that it would be brittle. In many agreements between the customer and smith for work, it was stipulated that the iron work was not to be done with stone coal. But, like all other improvements, it came into use gradually, and its superiority over charcoal for a high, quick heat, had to be established by experience. Another fact, equally patent, is, that no mechanic or artisan has been so completely put out of business, or his trade rendered almost next to useless by the invention of machinery as the blacksmith. Once, the most indispensable, now perhaps, his entire disappearance from the mechanical trades of the country, would produce the least inconvenience of any. Every article that the blacksmith was once looked to to make, is now produced by machinery, and can be bought much cheaper than it could be made by him.

OLD TIME WORKINGS.

The most distinguishing feature or characteristic of early pioneer days was the many social gatherings of neighbors for mutual assistance in the performance of labor too heavy for a single individual. The land was grown over with heavy timber and it all had to be cleared and fenced. One man could not manage the heavy logs alone, and so the neighbors would be informed that on a certain day they were to meet at this man's "new ground," and participate in a log-rolling and rail-splitting. Accordingly they all came with their axes and mauls. Some would be put to chopping down the trees, some to chopping off the cuts, some to splitting rails, and some to rolling together into large heaps such logs as would not split into rails. The boys would also come to pile, in large heaps, the brush and small limbs. These same brush heaps would, during the winter, become the roosting places of thousands of small birds, the killing of which, after dark, would afford a fine, but a very cruel sport for these same boys.

FIRE HUNTING.

But these heaps of brush, especially if they were cut and piled while the buds and leaves were on, afforded a far more exciting sport for the men, after night, than for the boys. When the leaves or buds had wilted in the hot sun, they gave forth a very sweet scent which was very enticing to deer in the vicinity of the "clearing," and they were attracted in great numbers by it. On dark nights, it was an easy matter, by means of a light or fire, to approach very near to these animals feeding on the wilted leaves, and shoot them. It was the custom to fire-hunt about these new grounds a great deal, and the hunters were usually quite successful, frequently killing several at one shot. One person would procure a shovel or pan of fire, and proceed a few feet in advance of the one with the gun, who would watch for the shining of the animal's eyes. For, when the men began to approach silently and cautiously, the deer would cease feeding, and gaze in astonishment, at the approaching light; and as soon as the eyes were seen, the hunter would fire, and generally, with effect. But, as the people began raising more cattle and sheep, it became too frequently the case that these domestic animals were more often killed than deer. Besides, careless or designing hunters were not so particular as to the kind of animal killed, so that it afforded meat; and, consequently, fire-hunting was eventually prohibited by law. Thus passed another very exciting, old-time sport.

HOUSE RAISINGS, ETC.

These men were strong and hardy, and the amount of work that was done at one of these "workings" would astonish people of the present day. It was a favorite occasion for the showing off of strength and general physical manhood, and many and severe were the tests to which the aspirants for honor were subjected. While there was generally plenty of home-made liquor on hand, and of which, each one usually partook quite freely, it was not the modern kind that takes the reason from the mind, and puts the devil into the heart. The utmost good humor prevailed, and, the funnier they became, the friendlier they were.

Or, it may have been a settler's cabin to be built; for, when a new family came into the neighborhood, the neighbors would all join in, and build them a house. This usually required two "workings." The first day they would go to the woods and get the logs ready. Some would chop down the trees; some would measure and cut off the logs; some would "scutch" the logs; and others would come along with a broadaxe, and hew two sides of the logs flat. The next day these logs would be hauled or dragged to the place where the cabin was to be built, and the "house-raising," would take place.

Four men would be selected to "carry up the corners," which consisted in notching and fitting the logs so that they would be close together, while the others would bring up the logs. This would continue until what we would consider a very low, one-story pen would be built. Then the end logs would be gradually shortened, and sloped, and the long poles to support the roof would be laid up instead of side logs. After these poles were all up, long, thin clap-boards would be put on, and heavy weight-poles would be used to hold them down, as there were no nails. In the meantime, some of the men had been splitting out logs into pieces four or five inches thick, for the floor. These were called puncheons, and were fitted in for the floor, making it as tight as possible. This much of the work usually constituted the day's work, leaving, for the man who was to occupy the house, the job of building a stick-and-mud chimney, to chink and daub the cracks, and to lay the hearth of flat stones. When the house was completed, the owner usually gave an old-fashioned party in honor of the friends whose kindness had furnished him a home.

The door of the primitive log cabin extended from the first log at the bottom to the top one, and was closed with a shutter made of puncheons similar to the floor, except they were thinner. These pieces were fastened together by wooden pins, and the door was hung with wooden hinges. The fireplace occupied the greater amount of the space of one end. When this was piled full of wood and set on fire, and a large pine knot thrown on, the room was sufficiently heated and lighted. These cabins were usually built near a good spring of water, and, in most cases, in the middle of the clearing, so that the approach of a bear, a wolf, or an Indian could be seen.

THE CORN HUSKING.

In the late fall, when the corn was ripe, and gathered in, there would be at each settler's cabin, another gathering of neighbors, this time, to help husk out the corn. This social function was a regular, annual feature, and was looked forward to with much interest. Much fun was, in some way or other, injected into the occasion. It was a custom rarely omitted to have a jug of corn juice placed in the center of the corn heap, and the crowd was divided into two equal divisions, and placed on opposite sides, and the race was to see which side would be the first to reach the jug. Other contests were to impose a fine of a gallon of "the article" on the one husking the fewest number of red ears.

THE QUILTING BEE.

Frequently, also, at the same time, the farmer's wife would embrace this occasion to have the ladies, young and old, of the neighborhood come and assist her in quilting a quilt. When the two affairs came off on the same day, the night would be most surely devoted to games, plays and dancing. In those days, everybody was invited, and everybody expected to come or render a good excuse at the first opportunity. If there happened to be some one in the neighborhood who was not deemed worthy to be invited, he construed it to mean that his permanent absence from that community would fill a long-felt want. It was also expected of a person having a "working," that he would, for the time at least, lay aside any little petty differences, or prejudice, that might exist between himself and a neighbor, and invite him along with the others. So, to a great extent, these gatherings were directly instrumental in wiping out old grudges and renewals of friendship. But as the people became more prosperous, they became more independent, and began drifting apart. Prosperity seems to breed selfishness, and degrades the social standard of the people. Later, I have seen the chasm between the people widened by differences in political and religious opinions to such an extent as to almost wipe out all reverence for the good old customs of the good old times of long ago. Schools and churches may increase, education and religion may become more widely diffused, but the world will never again witness the generosity, the hospitality, the unadulterated community of common interest, and common welfare, as that exhibited in the relations of pioneers to each other. The log cabin and the pioneer can never again be factors of our civilization. It is doubtful if history could ever repeat itself to the extent of their reproduction. There is no longer a westward march toward civilization, no longer a frontier. Alas! for the good old days of our grandparents. In those days a life seemed to count for much. All the power and influence of an individual seemed directed toward a worthy end, and left an impression, recognized and felt by every one. Now a life seems to be swallowed up and forgotten in the rushing, mighty whirl of these days of steam and electricity.

The plain, simple food, and the plain, simple dress, and the freedom from the worry and excitement induced by the fierce competition and rivalry, and the greed of fame and fortune, resulted in good health and long life to the people; and hence, with an undisturbed mind and body, and a full measure of days, they were enabled to more fully fulfil the great object of their existence on earth. The excesses and indulgences of modern times were the rarest exceptions. Though lacking much that we are disposed to call advantages, still what they accomplished must be considered something wonderful.

SCHOOL AND CHURCH--TEACHER AND PREACHER.

But the two institutions in which, next to their homes, the people felt the keenest interest, were the church and school. These buildings were built in easy reach of the entire community. Everybody was eager to lend a hand in their construction. In size they, especially the church, was some-what larger, and in general appearance more regard was had to neatness than the simple dwellings. The preacher and teacher, for the sake of economy, was generally combined in one individual, who, if he was not the head of a family in the community, usually boarded around among the patrons of his church and

48

school. He was, by virtue of his high and varied calling, an individual of no common importance. He received due credit for all the displays of the good qualities of his mind and heart. No one grudged his share of the meager contribution to the support of this distinguished and indispensable personage. His services did not come high, and he was content with very plain keeping in the way of food and raiment so long as he was accorded a hearty fireside welcome, and received the respect due one of his high station. Besides being the general adviser of the community in all things both spiritual and temporal, he was likewise the arbiter in matters of difference among the people, and from whose decision there was seldom an appeal. He taught school six days in the week, and preached on Sunday at the church. He also officiated as master of ceremonies at the weddings, and occupied a conspicuous seat at the table when the "infair" came off. He sang songs and offered prayers at the bedside of the sick and afflicted. And if, in response to his earnest petitions that the life of the sick one be spared, death finally closed the scene, he was given the credit of cheering the bed of death by glowing descriptions to the sufferer of a blissful immortality. At the grave, his voice in praise of the dead and in prayer for the living, as well as the old soul-stirring song, awakened the tenderest feelings, and disposed the minds of the listeners to the solemn reflections of the brevity of life, and the mystery and certainty of death.

THE SCHOOL.

His school duties consisted not only in hearing the childred read and spell, and in directing them in a few simple operations of "ciphering," but in making ink, shaping goosequills into pens, and ruling paper for copy books. His school sessions lasted nearly all day, and tardiness was treated as a crime. Order was maintained by mere physical force, and the rod was brought down with certainty and force on every offender, male or female, large or small, for the very slightest offence. If the child was spoiled, it was not from sparing the rod.

THE PREACHER.

His preaching, though delivered with simplicity, was yet vigorous and vehement. His sermons were not characterized by the breadth, scope, and variety as are those of modern days, but were selected from a comparatively limited range of subjects.

These were the Fall of Adam, the Flood, the Judgment, the Crucifixion and such others as would necessarily produce a considerable wave of feeling in the audience, to be strengthened and reinforced by the impassioned delivery of the preacher. No one was disappointed if he heard the same sermon, with slight variations three or four times in the course of a year's preaching. The efforts of the preacher seemed always actuated by practical considerations. Two things of the most overshadowing importance to his hearers were constantly impressed with the greatest vehemence and earnestness. One was the necessity of spiritual preparation in order to escape everlasting punishment, and the other was in order to reach heaven. In order to force the considerations home to the heart and conscience, he spared no words of horrible meaning in order to portray the untold agonies of hell, nor those of opposite import, to depict the priceless blessedness of heaven, with no thought that he was appealing to, stirring up, and encouraging only the most selfish motives. But after all, perhaps his preaching was most effective by virtue of this fact.

HARVESTING AND THRESHING.

The amount of wheat and oats raised in the early days of our country was very small compared with the present. But if the people were under the necessity of using the same methods of cutting their wheat, and cleaning out the grain, as were used fifty years ago, very little would be raised now. In those days, the grain was cut with a reap-hook. This was done by the person taking hold of as much of the straws as he could hold in his left hand, then using the reap-hook with his right hand, with a quick stroke, cut off the straws, and place them in bunches to be tied in bundles. The bundles were placed in shocks until thoroughly dry, then they were taken to the threshing-floor of the barn, and the heads all placed toward the center, and the butts outward. The grain was then beaten out with a hickory flail. Some used horses to tramp out the grain. The grain and chaff was then gathered up and poured into a fan mill and cleaned. This was a slow, laborious process, and it required so much time and labor that very little wheat was grown. Oats were fed in the sheaf, and only enough were threshed for seed. In time, the cradle was invented, and with this a good hand would cut from two to four acres a day. About the time the cradle came into use, some yankees invented a threshing machine. The first machine did not separate the grain from the chaff, and the fan mill was used the same as before. In a year or two, a machine was brought out that threshed and separated the grain. This machine marks the era of the wheat field. Wheat was no longer raised in patches, but fields were sown with it, as well as with oats. The reap-hook and the wooden flail were laid aside, and the darkeys had an easier time.

The meadows then consisted of a narrow level strip of land along the branch or creek. The grass was cut with an old Dutch scythe, that was sharpened on an iron stake driven into a stump or block, and beaten out with a hammer. This required to be done very frequently, and but little could be cut in a day. But as better blades were made with which to cut the grass, larger spaces were put in meadow, and more hay was raised. Later on, came the mowing machine, which did more to revolutionize farming than any one invention. The farmer then realized that any good land, no difference whether it was bottom land or not, would produce hay. Then he began to rest his land from corn by growing grass on it. Hay proved to be a great fattening food for stock, and was so much cheaper than corn that its use was very much increased. This resulted in the farmer keeping his cattle on the farm and fattening them on grass, and was the means of making far better times for him. The land was fresh and fertile, and produced abundant crops of corn, but it was not profitable to raise more than was needed for home use, as there was not much market for it. True enough, vast quantities of it was distilled into whiskey, but this article sold for fifty cents a gallon, and many farmers furnished the corn to the distiller and took a share of the product. The woods afforded acorns and chestnuts sufficient to fatten the hogs, and very little corn was fed to them. The great trouble was that there was so much woods that the hogs became wild, and late in the fall, the trouble of capturing and killing them was a tremendous job. Sometimes a farmer would bait his hogs at some point in the woods, and by feeding them with corn, get them sufficiently tame to entice them into a field with a strong, high fence, by scattering corn along, leading through a gap, and when all or several were inside, close up the gap, and begin the fun. This was a thrilling, but a very dangerous sport. The animals were very wild and vicious. When wounded or hemmed, they would charge upon their pursuers with a headlong dash, and nothing but a stroke sufficient to kill, would check them. It was folly to bring a dog among them; for as soon as he seized one of them, the whole herd would attack him and rip him literally into strings with their long tusks. They would sometimes attack a horse upon which the farmer was riding, and would sometimes be badly wounded despite his kicking. They were generally all shot that were sufficiently fat to be killed; then the smaller ones and the thin ones were turned back into the woods for another year.

It was often the case that these animals were so wild that they could no more be led into an enclosure than a drove of foxes. Then the sport took on a different form. They were hunted with dog and gun just as the bear was hunted, only it was more exciting and dangerous. The hunter would take his gun, mount his horse, call his dog, or dogs, and ride into the woods. He would soon either find a herd of hogs, or their sign. The dog was sent in pursuit, and would generally bay them in a short time. A bark or two was usually all the farmer heard; for at once, on sight of the dogs, the hogs would set up such a hideous, deafening grunting that they could be heard for two miles or more. The dog knew better than to catch one, for he would have been torn to pieces in a moment, but would run around the herd, keeping them in a dense mass, with their attention engaged until the hunter could ride near, dismount, and slip up in shooting distance, and perhaps shoot two or three before they would take alarm at the falling of their friends and break away. This was all that was attempted that day, or perhaps for a week until they would partially recover from their fright, and return to within a reasonable distance of the farmer's home. After shooting one or more of them, he would return, get assistance and bring his wagon, and haul in, and dress them. This would be repeated about every week until a sufficient supply of meat was secured. The hunter was careful to hitch his horse so as to reach him should the hogs perceive him, and make a dash for him, which they have been often known to do. Then the only means of escape was to reach the horse, or succeed in climbing a tree beyond their reach. They would often besiege the hunter up the tree for hours, grunting viciously.

Frequently farmers owning a drove of wild hogs would give permission, or engage the services of hunters by giving them half of all they would kill. These were a different species of hog from the kind now in the country. They were much taller and longer, and had long, slim noses and enormous tusks in the jaws. It was with great difficulty that a dog could catch one in a fair race. They were the terror of the woods, and would face any kind of enemy, and bears and wolves were careful not to attack the pigs while the old ones were near. The meat was much inferior to that of our present hog. It was tough and soon became strong and odorous. It lacked the tenderness and the juicy flavor of the meat of the present day.

MILLS.

The first saw mills, and indeed the only ones that were in the country until within the last thirty years were the old sash saws. It required a whole day to saw a large log into inch lumber. The machinery was very simple and cumber-some, but the arrangement for feeding and backing the log, was very ingenious for that day and time. In one of the early settlements there was a saw mill in a wild section of the country, on a creek, a mile or so from any dwellings. A man and his son were running the saw mill. As the saw cut so slowly, and as they were anxious to get all the lumber cut possible, they concluded when the noon hour arrived, to just sit on the log and eat their dinner, and let the sawing continue. While eating their dinner they spied a bear that had been attracted by the scent of the food, coming toward them.

They left the food on the log and sprang up into the saw-mill loft for safety. The bear, seeing the sudden disappearance of the men, and doubtless very hungry, came boldly into the mill, climbed up on the log, sat upright on his haunches, with his back to the saw, and began helping himself to the food. He was in the full enjoyment of meal, which he was devouring with a hearty relish, when the saw, which had been gradually creeping up to him, gave his back a cruel rake. The bear supposing no doubt that it was some one disputing his right to the dinner, in a fit of rage, whirled around just as the saw was coming down again, seized it in his teeth, and got his mouth very badly cut with the saw. Then realizing that a desperate battle was to be fought, the bear arose to his favorite fighting position, threw his arms around the saw, and with the next downward stroke was sawed nearly in two, and rolled off the log on the floor dead. The men had been watching the performance from the loft above, and now came down, skinned the bear, and carried his carcass home to be eaten by them, being well pleased with the exchange of their dinner for enough bear meat to last them for a week.

It was, as soon as practicable, the custom to have a saw mill in every community, and though the amount of lumber sawed was small, still it had a wonderful effect on building. The floors were made of planks; the doors were made of it; tables; shelves, and boxes were made of it; and the conveniences of the home were much increased by the use of lumber. Houses could be more easily and quickly built, and were much more tasty and comfortable. It is said that Gov. Blount imported weatherboarding from North Carolina, his former home, with which to encase the huge log mansion built for him in Knoxville.

The little "corn-crackers" were usually built at the same time and operated by the same power as the saw-mill. The mill-stones were of a very rough, inferior character, and the grinding was necessarily slow. The grist was almost invariably left at the mill for several days, the miller usually being able to guess with tolerable accuracy when it could be called for. It is related that a rather witty boy on calling for his meal, was informed that it was just put up for grinding, and that he could wait until it was

54

ground, and take it back with him. He concluded to do so. He stood by and watched the tiny, little stream of meal come out, and, at last, said to the miller, "I could eat this meal as fast as this mill can grind it. "How long could you eat it?" asked the miller. "Until I starved to death," answered the boy. Before these corn mills were built the people were subjected to the greatest inconvenience in order to procure bread. Many, indeed, did much of the time without it. Instead, corn was parched and eaten so, or the corn was pounded into meal, and baked into bread. Adam Meek, who settled about the year 1785, in the valley near Strawberry Plains, obtained his meal for a long time near Greeneville. But the early county records show that among the first acts of the county courts were premits to dam the creeks and erect mills. Knox county court was organized on June 16, 1792, and the records show that on the same day, Wm. Henry obtained leave to build a mill on Roseberry creek. Grainger county court was organized June 13,1796, and at this term of court, permits were issued to Nichols T. Perkins to erect a mill on Chamberlain, now Stiffey creek; to Wm. Thompson, on Buffalo creek; and to Wm. Stone, near the mouth of Richland creek. In the year 1786, a man by the name of Hazlitt built a mill on Beaver creek, near Mr. Meek. After six or seven years this was replaced by a better one built by James Walker. Adam Peck was the first settler on Mossy creek, and built a mill just below the present town in 1788. Some of these old time mills have been entirely destroyed, others have been rebuilt and equipped with modern milling machinery.

Before the settlers could obtain meal parched corn was a staple article of diet. On many of the long expeditions against the Indians the soldiers carred with them bags of parched corn, and slices of dried bear's or deer's flesh.

SALT.

Salt was for a long time a great luxury with the old settlers, and, as you may imagine, was difficult to obtain. People, on their hunting expeditions discovered trails leading or converging to a point, like the spokes of a wheel, and by following these trails, discovered that they lead to "salt licks." These salt licks were places where salt-water oozed from the ground, and to which the deer and buffalo would come to lick the salt. Hence, they were called "salt licks." The people boiled and evaporated this water, and thus obtained their first supplies of salt. The licks were the best places for the hunter to kill these animals. At the same time, other beings would know by instinct or experience, the same thing as the white hunter. The Indian had known, long before the white man, this favorite spot, and he, too, most likely, would be watching beside this same lick, and the white man would have to exercise the greatest caution, or he would receive a bullet that was at first intended by the Indian for a deer. When the Indians learned that the white men were hunting at the lick, they kept almost a continual watch on the trails that led to them, so that it became too dangerous for the settlers to hunt at them. The panther also knew that the deer would come to lick the salt-water and it was not an infrequent sight to see two or three of these ferocious brutes lying stretched on the limbs of as many trees, ready to spring on the unsuspecting animal that chanced to pass within reach. He, too, was a foe to be dreaded by the hunter; for such a mark for a rifle as he would make stretched out his full length on a horizontal limb, would constitute a temptation too strong to be resisted by the hunter. Stange as it may seem, more shots by an experienced hunter would result in wounding than in killing the animal; and then, unless badly crippled, he would make a ferocious assault on the hunter, who considered himself fortunate to escape with his life. If he did not have time to reload his gun, and the beast came on him, he would fight, using his gun barrel and large hunting knife.

THE WILD TURKEYS.

Another sport greatly relished by the early hunter was the hunting of wild turkeys. These large birds were eagerly sought for by the hunter as their flesh was exceptionally fine, and their feathers would make good pillows. One way of hunting them was to go out into the woods before daylight and listen for the gobble of the male or the loud twit of the hen. They came down from the roost about daybreak, and for several minutes would keep up almost a continual gobbling and twitting so that the hunter could approach the flock, and be ready to shoot one by the time it was light. They were quite easy to take alarm, and it was a difficult thing to approach them when they were scattered. The hunter would have but little hope of doing this, and would generally risk his chances by concealing himself and waiting until they fed within reach. As a rule, they would feed in one general direction and travel in this course for hours. So that a hunter would often climb high into a tree in order to watch them to find out which way they were traveling; and if going in an opposite direction, he would climb down from the tree, make a long circuit around them, and conceal himself in front of them.

Some hunters took a bone from the turkey's leg and made a kind of whistle with which they could imitate the gobble of a turkey, and could generally succeed in calling them up within shooting distance. The white man learned this from the Indian, and it was said that some of the Indians could use this deception so well that they could even beat the turkey at his own gobble. This device was a great advantage to the early hunter, and often enabled him to carry home a big fat turkey that he could have obtained in no other way. The Indian was not slow to learn the white man's fondness for turkey, and by means of his whistle, has enticed many a settler from his cabin, and lured him to his death. Often has a hunter taken down his gun on hearing the gobble of a turkey, as he supposed, and left his family in anticipation of a feast, never to again see his cabin.

In one of the western settlements was a man by the name of Castleman, who lived for a time with another settler whose name I can not recall. Castleman was an expert in the use of the turkey whistle and could imitate the birds almost perfectly, and at the same time could distinguish between the genuine sound and the imitation. He frequently remonstrated with the other settler who was disposed to hunt for every noise resembling that of a turkey. One day Castleman went out hunting alone and rather early. He had not been gone long before the other man heard, near his cabin, what he was sure was the gobble of a turkey. He took down his gun and went in the direction of the sound. Not long afterward, the sound of a gun was heard and the family expected him to return in due time with the turkey. Time passed, but he did not return, and they supposed that he had concluded to go on a farther hunt. About noon, Castleman returned, and, on inquiry, was told about the man going to find the turkey he had heard, of the firing of the gun, and was also informed of the strangest part of the affair, that the noise continued to be heard at the same place. Castleman stepped into the yard to listen, and sure enough, heard the sound, and rightly suspected the fate of his friend. He picked up his rifle, telling the family that he would kill that "turkey." Instead, however, of going in the direction whence the noise proceeded, he took a round-a-bout way, and came up behind the object of his hunt. The noise continued and he had no difficulty in locating it. He crept up softly, and saw by a stump, not a turkey, but an Indian, with his gun across the stump, watching in the direction of the cabin. A well directed shot from Castleman's rifle killed the savage, whose long hunting-knife was still covered with the blood of a recent scalp. Proceeding about fifty yards in the direction of the cabin, Castleman came across the dead body of his friend, pierced by the Indian's bullet. The Indian knew that there were two men belonging at the cabin, and was endeavoring to entice the other one out to be shot and scalped.

THE TURKEY PEN.

Besides hunting the wild turkey in the ways above mentioned, the old hunter frequently built what he termed a turkey-pen. First he dug a trench about two feet wide and about a foot and a half deep, gradually ascending until at the end of ten feet, it sloped up to the surface. The fresh dirt was removed or carefully covered over with dry leaves. A pen of fence rails, two or three feet high, was built over the last four or five feet of the ditch, and covered securely. Grain of some kind was then scattered in the ditch leading into the pen. The fowls would follow the grain into the pen, and they were safely imprisoned, for it never occurred to them to look downward, or to go out by way of the ditch. Often the entire flock was thus captured at one time.

EARLY ROADS.

The first roads in the newly settled country were narrow worn lanes, scarce two feet wide, lightly trodden over pine needles and fallen leaves among the tree trunks by the soft moccasined feet of the tawny savages as they silently walked in Indian file through the forests. These paths were soon deepened and worn bare by the heavy hobnailed shoes of the early settlers. Others were formed by the slow tread of domestic cattle, the best of all path-makers, as they wound around the hillsides to pasture or to drinking place. Then a scarcely broader bridle-path for horses, perhaps with blazed trees as guide posts, widened slowly to traveled roads and uneven cart ways. These roads followed and still wind today in the very lines of the footpath and the cattle track. Wet and marshy places were laid with poles cut in ten foot lengths and laid closely across the road. Some of these laid with pine poles served their purpose after a use of fifty years. They were called corduroy roads, and was the first effort at road improvement. The first turnpike in America was made when I was a small boy (1785-86) in Virginia, starting at Alexandria and extending down the Shenandoah Valley. It was at a tavern on this turnpike, while on a cattle drive to Petersburg, with my master, that I saw George Washington. I was a small boy, and did not then know how great a man he really was, but I well remember how he looked.

THE OLD-TIME WAGON.

I saw the first wagon ever used in the part of Virginia where I lived. It was the same kind as was first used everywhere in the new settlements where wagons were used at all. It was called the Conestoga wagon, that being the name of the place in Pennsylvania where they were first made. They were of the same general plan upon which wagons of the present day are made-- the difference consisting only in such improvements as have been made to render it less clumsy and more durable. Suitable iron was so scarce that not much of it was used on these old-time wagons. The axles were made of a tough, young pine sapling, which being daily greased with pine tar, became so tough and hard as not to need skeins, and would last for years without them. Very few of them had iron tires; and the first man to bring into the country about Blain's Cross Roads, in 1840, a wagon with tires made of iron, was, I believe, old Buckeye Crawford, who came from North Carolina, about that year, and settled by House Mountain. The hind wheels were much higher than they are now made; and, for a reason I never knew. The beds were very long, and were curved, being higher at each end than the middle. It took a blacksmith six weeks to make and iron one of these beds. They had no locks to these wagons, the convenient brake being an invention of the last forty years. A lock chain with a little fastening device was used, and a wheel was not merely checked in its speed, but locked fast. Consequently the tires would soon be ground into many thin places.

THE OLD-TIME STAGE COACH.

A Toast to the Old Stage Coach.

"Long ago, at the end of the route,
The stage pulled up, and the folks stepped out.
They have all passed under the tavern door--
The youth and his bride, and the gray three-score.
Their eyes were weary with dust and gleam,
The day had gone like an empty dream.
Soft may they slumber, and trouble no more
For their eager journey, its jolt and roar,
In the old coach over the mountain."

The writer finds that Uncle Pharaoh's description of the old-time stage coach in use when he was a boy, in the latter part of the eighteenth century, is almost identical with that given by Thomas Twining, an English writer, who traveled in New England in one of these vehicles in 1795. So, the latter's description is given.

"The vehicle was a long car with four benches. Three of these in the interior held nine passengers. A tenth passenger was seated by the driver on the front bench. A light roof was supported by eight slender pillars, four on each side. Three large leather curtains suspended to the roof, one at each side, and the third behind, were rolled up or lowered at the pleasure of the passengers. There was no place nor space for baggage, each person being expected to stow his things as he could, under his seat or legs. The entrance was in front, over the driver's bench. Of course the three passengers on the back seat were obliged to crawl across all the other benches in order to get to their places. There were no backs to the benches to support and relieve us during a rough and fatiguing journey over a newly and ill-made road."

The vehicle was called a stage coach because the distance between the stations on the route were called stages; and usually a fresh relay of horses was in readiness at each station. The distance between New York and Philadelphia is two hundred and ninety-seven miles, and in 1812, it took six days to make the journey by stage coach. The fare for each passenger was twenty dollars, besides way-expenses of seven dollars more. The expense by wagon was five dollars a hundred weight for persons and property, and the way-expenses were twelve dollars, for it took twenty days. Each station was an inn, or ordinary, and afforded accommodations for the passengers, at a moderate expense. Not only did these afford food and lodging for the traveler, but he could also procure, if he chose to do so--and he usually did--almost any kind of drink which suited his taste. These various drinks were made of home products, and mixed under various names.

THE OLD-TIME TAVERN, OR ORDINARY.

As has been stated, these taverns were located on the stage routes, and were usually a day's journey apart, so that rest could be afforded for the horses, and food and shelter for the traveler. Encouragement and protection were afforded these houses of entertainment by the county courts; and no one was permitted to open and run an establishment of the kind without a license. The prices to be charged for meals and drinks was fixed by law; and, in some places, the number of drinks to each person, were limited, in order to control drunkenness.

Very stringent restrictions were placed on landlords in regard to the keeping of strangers. The names of these were given to the town authorities, who could, if they saw fit, warn such persons to leave at once, as might appear to be of a suspicious character, or whose presence at the place might be considered as dangerous or undesirable. In case action was taken, a record was made of it. Our ancestors were kind and hospitable to the worthy, but sternly intolerant of wrong-doers, or even of those suspected of evil intentions. Landlords were closely watched, and held strictly accountable, under heavy penalties, for the conduct of travelers or other persons frequenting their place. No loud singing, dancing, or other boisterous noises were allowed. Drunkenness was strictly forbidden, and landlords were subject to have their license revoked, and heavy fines imposed, who allowed such conduct. A favorite location for the tavern was at a ferry; and the landlord who was so fortunate as to control the patronage of a tavern and a ferry, held a position truly envied by his less fortunate neighbors, and was sure of a competence not afforded by any other calling of that day.

The better class of old-time taverns always had a parlor. This was used as a sitting room for women travelers, or might be hired for the exclusive use of one wealthy person or family. It was not so jovial a room as the tap-room, where the drinks were dispensed, though in winter, an open fireplace gave to the formal furnishings that look of good cheer and warmth and welcome which is ever present, even in the meanest apartment, when from the great logs the flames shot up glowing and crackling. We are more comfortable now, with our modern ways of house-heating, but our rooms do not look as warm as when we had the old open fireplace.

The tap room was usually the largest room of the tavern. It had universally a great fireplace, a bare, sanded floor, and ample seats and chairs. It often had, also, a rather tall, rude writing desk, at which a traveler might write a letter or sign a contract, and where the landlord made out his bills and kept his books. But the principal feature of this room was the various kinds of drinks made and sold there.

RAILROADS.

No railroads were built in lower Virginia before the time we left there to come to East Tennessee (about 1838), but several short lines of road had been built in the mining regions of Pennsylvania, and were in operation then. I never saw these railroads, but well remember the descriptions given me of them, by persons who had seen them.

The track consisted of pieces of timber with strap iron spiked down on top of them. These spikes would soon come loose, and the ends of the straps would turn up, and were called "snake-heads." These snake-heads were sometimes forced up through the cars, and did great damage. Snake-heads were as common in early railroading as snags were in early steamboating. Scarcely was a trip ever made that some serious accident of some kind did not occur. Few of these mishaps were fatal to life, but they generally resulted in crippling the machinery so that horses or oxen, often both, had to be impressed in order to drag the clumsy locomotive and its load to the nearest station for repairs. The brakes were very poor and would not stop the train. When they came to a station, the engineer opened the safety valve and allowed the steam to escape, two big negroes would seize the end of the train, and hold it, while timbers would be placed across the track in front of the wheels. Both the engineer and the conductor favored a curved track in order that they might look back and see that everything was all right.

A YEAR WITH NO SUMMER (1816).

We call this (1901-2) a long, hard winter, but I remember a winter in Old Virginia, when I was a young man, that far surpassed any winter remembered by the oldest inhabitants. I heard the people here in East Tennessee speak of it after I came here over twenty years afterward. The winter of 1815 had been, as was then usual, a very severe one, and the cold frozen weather extended far into the new year. When time came for gardening in the spring, the fury of winter had not abated in the least. In April, the snow was from four to six feet deep. In May, the surface only had melted, and the ground could not be reached for planting purposes. In June, the snow had melted, but the ground was still frozen hard, and toward the end of the month another snow had fallen, sufficiently for sleighing purposes, and lasted for days.

On the morning of July 4, the water froze in the wells and pitchers of the early settlers, and there was excellent skating in the neighborhood ponds. Snow fell toward noon, and the usual Independence Day exercises were held in an old-time log church, warmed by blazing log fires, and participated in by men, women and children clad in mid-winter clothing.

The spring, when it came in reality, was so short and severe that no vegetation could grow in it. In August, the corn that had struggled against the adverse conditions of climate, went to tassel so early that it was useless for anything except fodder. In the spring of 1817, farmers were obliged to pay unheard-of prices for seed corn raised in 1815. All kinds of breadstuffs went up until flour brought $17.00 a barrel.

The winter following, as well as that preceding this remarkable summer, was likewise one of intense cold. All the streams were frozen over solid, and the usual hauling was done over the ice the same as on the land. The public health, however, was never better, and though the crops were a failure, the old-time settler did not lose spirit, or become discouraged.

There never was such a time before or since for hunting deer. The snow had frozen so that a crust was formed on top that would hold up the weight of the dogs, but the sharp feet of the deer would break through, and they could not escape their pursuers, and so they were nearly all killed. They were never afterward very plentiful except in the mountains. Their flesh, however, was not very good, as they had become poor through starvation, but were hunted and killed for mere sport. Many domestic animals likewise perished from cold and hunger. No, sir, our winters now do not compare with the old-time winters. They have been becoming milder for a hundred years or more.

TRIP TO THE WESTERN DISTRICT.

Old Master Jackson was very rich, and when he became very old, and thought he was soon going to die, he decided to divide his money and property among his children. His three daughters, and as he then thought, his other son, Sandy Jackson, were living in the far western part of the state. He concluded to send Master Corbin Jackson and myself with a wagon to the Western District to bring home his children.

The government of North Carolina had commissioned a party of men to look out, survey, and clear out a road leading from the lower end of Clinch mountain, through Nashville to the Cumberland settlements. This road is now, and has ever since been called the Emory road, and was the only road deserving the name, leading from East Tennessee into the then far west. This road was made so that emigrants from Virginia, North Carolina, and upper East Tennessee could reach the western part of the state which was being rapidly settled up. But making a road then and now, are widely different. Then making a road meant the clearing out of the trees, logs, and larger stones from a strip of land through the woods, from ten to twenty feet wide. No ditching or grading was done, and the gulleys were filled in with logs or stones so that a traveler's wagon could cross.

Any person who has traveled this road for any considerable distance can not fail to notice that the land on which the road was made, was not well chosen. It often winds over high hills, often making curves in order to do so, when it could have gone around them. As a reason for this, I was told that those men who looked out the road often followed Indian trails which generally led over high hills in order for the Indians to take frequent views of the surrounding country, in their travels. They seemed to have had in mind the crossing of the streams, for the road usually leads to shallow places in the creeks and rivers, where fords were made by cleaning out the largest stones. As there were no railroads leading into the western country, we were obliged to make our trip over this road, and in many places, far from settlements, it was very bad indeed. Streams had washed across it and cut such gulleys that we had to fill them up, or to make a kind of bridge in order to cross. In some places, especially in the mountains, it had overgrown with bushes so that we had to use our axe. We had frequent trouble in trying to ford the streams that would get so full from the rains, besides, we did not know, and sometimes could not tell, just where the ford was.

We started from Blain's Cross Roads at the lower end of Clinch Mountain in October, and the weather was quite cool. Our traveling outfit was an old-fashioned covered wagon, pulled by two large horses, a bay and a black. It was a heavy, tar skein wagon, and required to be greased with pine tar grease every day. So I provided a large bucket full, hung underneath the wagon, to the tail pole. There was an old-fashioned feed-box to the hind gate of the wagon, where the horses were hitched to eat their noon meal. We also took with us sufficient quilts and blankets to keep us warm. Whenever we would happen to reach a settler's house about camping time, Mr. Jackson would generally sleep in the house, but I never slept in a house during the trip. I would always sleep in the wagon whether he was with me or not. We were afraid thieves would try to steal our horses and rob our wagon; and many times the two large, fierce dogs we took with us would set up a furious barking, and more than once, on slipping out to our horses, have seen a man glide away among the trees, and disappear in the shadows. Sometimes one or more suspicious looking men would come around to our camp, apparently to talk, but we eyed them closed, and fancied we could detect them eyeing the place where, and the way we had fastened our horses. We would always try, in some way, to let them know that we were armed, and would defend ourselves. We gave, also, some great accounts of our dogs, how vicious they were.

We would always build a large log fire when we camped for the night. This not only kept us warm, but served to keep away wildcats, bears and wolves that would be sure to prowl around our camp at night. Very often we would be awakened in the late hours of the night by the fierce barking of our dogs as though some human or animal was approaching our wagon, which we knew was the case, and although we frequently heard retreating footsteps in the woods, we seldom saw anything, and never knew for sure whether it was man or beast. And while we did not live in particular dread of any danger, still we knew that we were just as liable to attack from one as form the other, and were always on our guard.

Mr. Jackson and I were both very fond of broiled meat, and when we began cooking our meat over the fire, the scent of the scorching meat would be certain to attract any bear or wolf, or especially any wild cat that might be prowling about in the vicinity. These latter would come very near to our camps giving forth their vicious yells, until, at times, they seemed to be on every spur of the ridge or mountain. We did not care much for them, for we felt sure that our dogs and fire would keep them at a safe distance. We were not so positive, however, as to the wolves, which we knew went in packs, and when driven by hunger, would not hesitate to attack a whole wagon train. We only heard a few solitary howls from these savage brutes, and when they seemed to be rather close to our camp, we would discharge our pistols, and on hearing their howls, our dogs would begin barking furiously, and the stragglers would depart, not, however, until they had climbed to the highest ridge at hand, and given several savage howls, as if to summon help from a distance. But once we had a serenade from a panther which tried our nerves, and made the hair stand on end. This was when we encamped at the foot of Cumberland Mountain. It was a wild, desolate place, where several spurs of the mountain reached down to the road where we fixed our camp. We had tied and fed our horses, cut some dry wood and made a rousing fire--for the evening was chilly--and began broiling our meat, when a scream, resembling that of a woman, in distress, was heard, on a spur of the mountain not a quarter of a mile distant. The first yell convinced me what it was, but Mr. Jackson insisted that it was a wolf. After about five minutes, another unearthly scream rent the still and solemn night. This time it was not more than half as far away, and our dogs were terribly excited, and seemed to be actually frightened.

After a few minutes the scream again broke upon our frightened ears, this time very close to us, but he had changed from a direct course toward us, and had crossed over to another spur, and we could hear him walking in the leaves. Our dogs had taken refuge under the wagon, and it was with great difficulty that we could induce them to come out. One of us got the axe, and another the large pistol we had with us, and prepared for a desperate fight, thinking that he meant to attack us. But he went nearly around us, keeping about the same distance away, and disappeared in the opposite direction. We were glad when he left us. One who has once heard the scream of a panther is not likely to ever forget it, nor to ever want to hear it again. We were told by the settlers about the mountains, that these animals were very bold, and would come into the barnyard and carry off pigs and lambs, and had been known to spring on a child and carry it off and devour it. Their favorite method was to climb a stooping tree, or lie flat on a limb near a path where cattle, sheep or hogs were accustomed to pass, and to pounce down upon them. When cornered, they fight desperately and easily whip off a whole pack of dogs, frequently killing several of them.

It took us a whole day to cross the mountain, and we camped at a cabin on the other side. Mr. Jackson slept in the cabin, and I slept in the wagon. That night we were not disturbed. On the next night, we reached a house and, as usual, Mr. Jackson stayed in the house. It had been raining a great deal that day, and continued raining at night. We got shelter for our horses, and I brought my quilts in, and slept on the porch, the dogs staying with the wagon. Next morning I was awakened by something sharp being poked against me. When I aroused up, there stood about a dozen regular soldiers about me. They had poked me with their sharp sabres. I was terribly scared at first to see the glittering guns and sabres, and the blue uniforms of the soldiers. They all wore high top boots, and big spurs. They asked me what was I doing there, where was I from, where was I going, and who was with me. I was trying to get my senses together enough so that I could tell them, when Mr. Jackson came out. They then left me alone and began questioning him. He answered a few questions--what he thought was proper, and enough for them to know--and then told them that he knew his business and could take care of himself and did not need their protection, which seemed to make them somewhat angry. He generally wore a cap in the house, and he had it on while he was talking to them. This cap seemed to amuse them very much, and they poked it with their swords and asked him what it was. This made him very angry, and finally, when they went away and left us, he pointed to his pistol, as much as to say that he would use it on them if they bothered him any more; but he did not think of it while they were there.

We drove on, and met them twice that day, and they passed us twice going in our direction. They were well mounted, and each one carried his gun across his saddle in front of him. They seemed to be guarding about ten miles of the road, but we could not find out their business.

After crossing the mountains nearly everybody we talked to told of the dreadful crimes of the nortorious Tennessee outlaw, John A. Murrell. He had been stealing slaves, robbing and murdering in all the western part of the country. I was almost scared to death for fear he would run on to us, and take me off. Mr. Jackson, seeing how badly frightened I was, thought to have much fun out of me, and told me many horrible things he had read and heard of Old Murrell, in order to work on my fears. He told me of his meeting with a stock driver, once, and turning and traveling with him until they came to a spring. They got down to get water. The stock driver lay down to drink, and Murrell shot him. He robbed his pockets and only found seventy-five cents. He afterward said that a man that dressed as fine as that man did, and pretended to be a stock driver, and had no more money than that, ought to be killed.

He also told me of his having stolen a certain old negro man and sold him ten times, each time the old slave would run away, come back to Old Murrell who would give him ten dollars. He said that Murrell had a secret cave where he put the negroes and horses he stole until he would have a boat load, when he would take them down the Mississippi river, to New Orleans, and sell them. But before we reached Nashville, we learned that Murrell had been captured, convicted and sent to the penitentiary. This was most welcome news to me, but, somehow, I could not help feeling afraid, lest he should escape from the prison and take me in. But I had the great satisfaction, as well as my curiosity satisfied to see the very man himself in chains. We had to pass right by where the convicts were at work, and seeing an ugly looking man with a ball and chain around his leg, working in a blacksmith shop, I asked who it was, and was told that it was the notorious outlaw, John A. Murrell. Then I ventured up and took a close look at him, and felt just about as one feels when looking at a lion in a cage. He seemed to be sullen, and did not like being looked at. I wanted to remember his features so that if he ever escaped, and took up his old trade, and I saw him, I could keep out of his way.

It was a considerable distance beyond Nashville to where the children were, but the roads were better, and we made better time. The name of the place was Green Garden. We put up with a man by the name of Lewis Lane. I was sent with the horses to the stable, and was told to feed them. I started to give the horses some corn, but the man called out to me to let that corn alone, and to go down into the field and get some dry stalks. We found that feed was scarce in that neighborhood, and very hard to get.

It took us about two days to hunt up the girls, and learned that Sandy Jackson had gone to New Orleans. Mr. Jackson wanted to find him very much, and talked of leaving me there, and going to New Orleans to get him. But I was so averse to remaining in that neighborhood, that he was afraid I would run off and come back to East Tennessee and leave him and the girls. So, he decided that we would come back, and write for him to come.

70

After resting our horses a few days, we started on our homeward journey. It had taken us ten days to make the trip out, and as we had a much heavier load back, we supposed it would take us longer, but we made the trip back in the same number of days. In going out, we had learned where the houses were on the road, and Mr. Jackson had made arrangements for lodging for the girls, and so we regulated our travel back so as to reach the houses at night. Sometimes we would reach them before dark, and sometimes a while after dark. The girls would stay in the houses, and when Mr. Jackson could not get lodging, he would stay in the wagon with me.

On the way back we experienced an awful storm. One day it had rained more or less all day, and toward night it began to look like a storm would come. We urged our team on as fast as possible so as to reach the house of a widow woman, where we had secured lodging as we went out.

We reached the place just before dark, and barely had time to put up the horses, and fasten down the wagon cover when the storm began coming on.

I got into the wagon, and began covering myself up, when the dogs under the wagon began barking. I heard some one coming toward where I was, and spoke to the dogs to be quiet. Two women from the house came, and climbed upon the wagon tongue, and asked me to go to the house. I told them I would stay with the wagon. They then asked me to come to the house and get something to eat. I told them that I had plenty. They begged me to go to the house and get some more quilts to put over me. I told them I had plenty of cover. Seeing that they could not get me to leave the wagon at all, they left and went back to the house. Very soon it began thundering and lightning such as I had never seen before, and have never seen since. It seemed that the thunder would jar down the houses and trees. The lightning was so steady and constant that you could see an object as well as in daylight. It just seemed that the whole world was on fire. For the first time, the dogs left the wagon, and went to the stable where the horses were. I expected every moment that the lightning would tear the wagon to pieces. I was never, in all my life, so scared. I never expected to live through it, and wished that I had gone to the house with the women. I suppose the thunder and lightning lasted about an hour--it seemed to me four--when the rain began pouring in torrents. It seemed like dashing from a bucket, and I peeped out from under the cover to see what the storm had left, and the earth appeared as a sheet of water. The mountain creeks could be heard roaring for miles in all directions. When the rain was over, I got out of the wagon to look around, and the people came out from the house to see what had become of me, and were much surprised to see me safe and sound. We next thought of our horses. I took a pine torch and went to the stable, and found them and the dogs all right. Next morning we were not in a hurry to start, thinking to allow time for the streams to run down, and supposing that the roads would be repaired from the washouts, by people along the road who had to use it. Mr. Jackson ordered a ham to be boiled for us to use on the way back home. He especially requested that it be cooked well done, as the girls could not eat it if it was not done. When we went to use some of it for dinner we found that it had just been put into boiling water and taken out, and was not cooked at all. Mr. Jackson and the girls were very angry, but if they had looked closely at Pharaoh, they would have seen a smile bloom out on his face, for he knew that the most of that ham would fall to his share. And sure enough it did, and I had a fine time the balance of the way home broiling and eating ham. After twenty days absence, we arrived back at Blain's Cross Roads. The trip had been the longest and the most interesting one of my whole life. I had enjoyed the greater part of it, and had been pretty badly scared on several occasions. It proved too hard a trip on our stock. Our big black horse suffered the most. After we came back, the hair all came off his body, and he soon died. It seems to me now hardly possible that any team of horses could ever stand such a trip. People of the present day, who now travel in modern conveyances over the same road we traveled, could never be made to realize by any description, the inconveniences of travel by the means and the conditions of the same sixty years ago.

PHARAOH'S MASTER--PRACTICAL JOKES. FREE MASONRY.

Master Corbin Jackson was a jolly, good-natured fellow, and when in a good humor, he delighted to play practical jokes on me. I generally enjoyed them, as they usually afforded me considerable fun; but sometimes they were rather tough on me, and I got the worst end of the joke. The one that I am now going to relate did not terminate just as he intended that it should. Mr. Jackson was a Mason, and one day he was telling me what a great thing Free Masonry was for him, and said he did not see why it should not be just as good for me as for him. I told him that it looked that way to me. He said that if I wished to become a Mason he would initiate me free of any charge, although it had cost him a great deal of money. I agreed to allow him to proceed with the ceremony of making me a Mason; and he said we would go into the next room. He took a key out of his pocket, and I asked him what it was; and he said it was a "Chris Key," used in initiating people. I asked him what was he going to do with it, and he said he would have to use it on me. He told me to lie down before the fire, face downward, and to bare my back, as he would have to press it against the skin on my back. Just then I heard the key strike the andiron, and the truth flashed across my mind--he was heating the key. I jumped to my feet just as he was about to brand my back with a hot key. He said I would never make a Mason, and I told him not if I had to have my back burned.

HIDING THE KNIVES.

But the next joke he played on me succeeded better to his liking and worse to mine. This time he had studied up a sure enough plan to burn me. He sent me to the kitchen for three table knives, and proposed to me that I might go outside and hide them, taking one at a time; and, in case he did not remain in the house and tell me where I put the last one, that he would give me a plug of tobacco. I, of course, agreed to make the trial, little suspecting that a hard joke was in the game. He handed me one of the knives which I carried out and concealed. I returned to the room, and he handed me another one which I likewise took out and hid. But when I came back and he handed me the third one, the blade was so hot that it burned my fingers, and I dropped it on the floor at his feet. He called out, "There, Pharaoh, is the knife," and fairly shook with laughter. Quick as a flash, I grabbed up the knife by the handle, which was cool, and sprang out and hid it. He claimed that I was beaten, and I claimed I was not, for I had them all hidden. I would not tell him where they were until he gave me the tobacco. So, after all, I came out fairly well in the joke, even if I did get my fingers burned.

I could tell many more, but these will be sufficient to show the jolly, good time we had.

POLK AND JONES DEBATE AT BLAIN'S X ROADS.

One of the most memorable times that ever occurred at Blain's X Roads, was the occasion of the great debate between James K. Polk and James C. Jones, candidates for governor, over sixty years ago.

It was a time of great political excitement, and party spirit was running very high. It was the beginning of the practice of what was called stump-speaking, which afterward became so popular. It was called stump-speaking for the reason that the candidates more often spoke in the open air than in a building, and frequently mounted on stumps or empty boxes so as to be seen by their hearers. The two parties, on this occasion, were about equally divided, and about the only way to distinguish between them, was that the Whigs usually wore a coon-skin cap--a coon skin being an emblem of the Whigs--while the Democrats could be generally recognized by their yelling. Such an occasion was also the favorite resort of horse jockeys, shooting matches, and frequently a muster in the forenoon. Hence, there was most sure to be a large, miscellaneous assemblage from a radius of several miles around. Plenty of pure, home-distilled whiskey and brandy, and an abundance of hard cider and ginger cakes was always on hand. It was a genuine old-fashioned, go-as-you-please day, when every man was considered as having equal rights and privileges, which was construed to mean the right to get drunk and whip whomsoever he was able. But fighting then, was not as it is now. A man who would use a rock, stick, club, knife or gun in a fight, was regarded as a coward, and no one would have anything to do with him. The combatants used their fists, and when a man "got enough," he said so, and the fighting stopped, the whipped man set up the treat, and no thought of renewing the trouble at any other time or place, was ever indulged. In fact, the fighters were afterward generally the best of friends. Such conflicts were always expected, and usually occurred on such occasions, but were never seriously considered.

Well, the immense crowd had been gathering since early morning, and by noon it resembled a small army. There had been, in the forenoon, the usual horse swapping, match shooting, dog fighting, and fisticuffs, but the crowd was, in the main, in a jolly, good humor, everybody having had a regular picnic. Now it was time to begin looking for the speakers and a change of program. There was no railroad then, and the candidates were to come on the regular stage coach from Knoxville, which was due to arrive about noon. So, all eyes were turned down the road to catch a first glimpse of the incoming coach. They were not doomed to wait very long, for it soon came into view over the hill, and Mr. Samuel Croft, the veteran stage driver, blew a stirring blast upon his bugle, as was his custom.

Then, the air resounded with deafening cheers for Polk and Jones, as they were supposed to be in the coach. When the coach came to a standstill and the speakers alighted, there was more hurrahing and a general hand shaking. Most of the people did not know one from the other until the time for speaking, and their names were called. A speaker's stand and a few rude seats had been constructed on a little round knoll in a grove of timber just east of the road; and, as it was time for speaking to begin, the candidates repaired to it. Polk was introduced as the first speaker, and took the stand amid the thunders of applause from his friends. He was a gentleman of fine appearance, tall and handsome, an eagle black eye--deep and penetrating, had a splendid voice, and spoke with telling effect. He discussed, in an able manner, the leading political issues, and then paid his respects to his opponent, using many amusing jokes and anecdotes. He referred to Jones as "Lean Jimmy," and characterized his followers as the "coon-skin constituency." His speech was a masterly effort, and was all his friends could wish. When he took his seat, it was the general impression throughout the crowd that the Democrats had carried the day.

When Jones arose to speak it was in a somewhat hesitating manner, which did not afford promise of a satisfactory effort. He, by no means, possessed the prepossessing appearance of his opponent. He was six feet two inches tall, and weighed only one hundred and twenty-five pounds. His face was by no means beautiful to behold, and to say that the Whigs were considerably taken back by the personal appearance of their candidate, would be stating the case none too strongly. Then, again, their ardor was very much cooled by his awkward, hesitating manner. However, they rallied sufficiently to give him a few rousing cheers, to be followed by the hisses of the Democrats. After the usual formal salutation, he stood silent, fumbling in his side pocket, apparently, as all thought, for his handkerchief; but, behold! instead, what should he fish out but a piece of coon-skin, about four by six inches, and holding it up in full view of the large crowd, stroked it's fur, and said in a loud, clear voice, "Was there ever finer fur than this?" This was enough. A thunderbolt in a clear sky, would not have produced greater excitement, or scarcely more noise. Instantly, the coon-skin caps were as thick in the sky as stars on a clear night. The shouts and yells from the Whigs was truly deafening. A regular panic ensued, which for a time resembled a young riot. It was fully thirty minutes before enough quiet was restored for the speaker to proceed. When finally, he was allowed to go on it was evident that he was perfectly at ease, and had the situation fully at his command. He was, no doubt conscious of his inability to cope with Polk in serious debate, but he answered briefly, and to the satisfaction of his friends, the arguments of Polk. He turned all of that speaker's jokes against him, making of them, the most amusing and ridiculous applications. He then added many of the drollest and most laughable anecdotes ever heard, and kept the crowd. Democrats as well as Whigs, in a continuous uproar of laughter, from start to finish. Both sides naturally claimed to have carried the day. It was certainly a glorious day for Blain's X Roads, and she never had another such a grand occasion.

The result of this memorable campaign in Tennessee is well known. Jones was elected by a large majority. This was in 1841. Again in 1843, he defeated Polk a second time by much the same tactics. But James K. Polk was the idol of Tennessee Democrats, and was nominated, in 1844, for President. Though failing to carry his own state, which was still dominated by "Lean Jimmy's Coon-Skin Constituency," he was nevertheless elected over Henry Clay, the Whig candidate.

JOHN CHESNEY, PHARAOH'S LAST MASTER.

John Chesney, one of the earliest settlers on Bull Run Creek, was born at Spartanburg, South Carolina, December 5, 1794, and emigrated, early in the century, to East Tennessee. He was scarcely grown when he came, and was accompanied by his father and mother. It appears that his father did not possess the energy and ambition necessary to conquer a wilderness and build up a new home. So these arduous duties devolved upon the son and mother, who proved themselves equal to the occasion. The young man acquired a large body of land on Bull Run Creek and Comb ridge. Of the latter, he and William Colvin, bought a section extending about seven miles, for fifty dollars apiece. By the time Mr. Chesney had his home well under way, he had three neighbors--James Salling, above Maynardville; Mr. Cannon, at the lower end of Clinch mountain, and William Lane, about a mile above Cedar Ford. Soon Mr. Wyrick settled just above him on the same creek, and ere long the settlement was augmented by other settlers coming in. Mr. Chesney built a mill on the creek, and also operated a distillery. He was a soldier in the War of 1812, and served with Gen. Jackson. He married Ruthie, daughter of Wm. Lane, one of the earliest settlers. He died June 15, 1876, and was buried in the old family grave yard, in sight of where he built his first house.

Upon asking Mr. Tilmon Chesney, a son of our sketch, why his father, as well as many of the other old settlers, passed over the comparatively level country, extending south and west of the lower end of Clinch mountain, and making their settlements in the rough, hilly portions, I was told by, him--and the same was afterward corroborated by other pioneers--that these smoother portions were covered with a dense growth of wild pea vine, and the lower districts, with an almost impenetrable cane brake. This land had but very little timber then, and was known as The Barrens. These cane brakes were exceedingly difficult to prepare for the cultivation of a corn crop. The pea vines furnished the most excellent pasture for the cattle and hogs, and seemed designed by nature to serve this purpose to the early settler while he was devoting his cleared land to the raising of corn. But this wholesale pasturing by the immense numbers of cattle, sheep and hogs, at the early season of the year, before the seed pods matured, caused succeeding crops of this wild forage to become lighter and lighter; and since it propagated entirely by means of seed, it soon became extinct. But in its place bushes sprang up, and in the course of half a century, a splendid growth of forest timber covered the Barrens; and they, too, are a thing of the past--gone, save in the memory of the pioneer.

Since the writer has been accorded the inestimable privilege of recording the recollections of Mr. Chesney's old exslave, Pharaoh, who has lived to become the most remarkable character, perhaps, on the American continent, he does not deem out of place, an incident or two of the old man's life, rather amusing, but interesting.

As has been stated, Mr. Chesney had a distillery in which was made the old-time, pure, unadulterated corn, apple, and peach juice, but known then as now, by familiar names. Uncle Pharaoh was not averse to taking a drink of these spirits when occasion presented. Neither was Billy Hart, a diminutive specimen of manhood who lived with Mr. Chesney, and who, from the small size of his feet, is now remembered by the name of "Dollar Foot." On one occasion, Pharaoh and Billy had been sent with two pails of slop quite a little distance away, to feed the hogs. It seems that each of them had been imbibing too freely, but succeeded in reaching the pen, climbing over, and pouring out the slop. While in the pen, they began scuffling, and Billy becoming angered, began fighting Pharaoh. The latter being very strong, picked up the little fellow and pitched him outside the pen. Billy whimpered and threatened to tell the darkey's master for throwing him out. Whereupon Pharaoh jumped out, picked him up, and threw him back in, saying as he did so, "Now, what ye gwine to tell him?"

A NARROW ESCAPE.

Mr. Chesney's mill was built on Bull Run creek, the dam extending across. When the creek became swollen from heavy rains, such quantities of logs and brush came down as to endanger the safety of the mill, and Pharaoh was generally put to watch and keep these drifts pushed away. On one occasion the creek was very full, and as there had been so much clearing along the little bottoms, immense drifts of brush, trees, and logs were rusing down over the dam. Pharaoh, armed with a long spike pole, was standing on the forebay, pushing away such objects as threatened to strike the mill. As a large log came rolling along in the mad rushing current, he made a punch at the log, but his aim was not good. His pole missed the log and he could not recover the inertia of his body, and went plunging head first into the roaring, rushing tide. Over the dam he went, and struck the surging, splashing foam under the immense sheet of water along with the log he had aimed at. He was ducked and soused and pitched and tossed about until he was more dead than alive, but finally succeeded in getting to the shore. He crawled out and went shivering and dripping to the house, walked up to the door, and said, "Massa, I s'pose you don't know how near you came losin' dis nigger a while ago."

SLAVES AND SLAVERY.

There were good slaves and bad slaves, and there were good masters and bad masters. There is an old saying that, "Bad fences make roguish cattle," and I have often thought that bad slaves often made bad masters. Slaves were often punished, sometimes severely, but as a general rule they deserved all that was given them. Many slaves seemed to think of only how they could shirk the tasks that were given them to do, and to kill all time possible, and where you knew such as these you would often hear of whippings. I was not surprised when I heard about it, but more so, that I did not hear of it oftener. The darkey who went about his work in a cheerful, good-humored way, and tried to do his work right, and to please his master was sure to have a good time, and seldom got a punishment. But the one who was

80

slow, and sullen, and slighted his work would be most sure to have a rough time. Sometimes when a darkey would not work he was put on short rations for a day or two, and this would generally bring him to his senses sooner than a whipping. All the talk you hear about masters starving their slaves is bosh, for a man with any sense would know that a starved negro like a starved horse could not work; and, as work was what they were kept for, they were, of course, kept in condition to work. I was a slave for eighty years, and I have seen all kinds of slaves and all kinds of masters; and in nearly every case it was as I have said. Of course, I have known exceptions where slaves were cruelly and inhumanly treated. I have known them punished by standing them on hot irons; by tieing their hands and feet, and laying them down in the hot sun; by starving them; and by whipping their naked backs with a bundle of raw-hide strings. True enough, these were generally very unruly slaves, but the punishment was unreasonable, and it only made the slave more sullen, and indifferent to his master's interests. Certain classes of white people living in a neighborhood would often get slaves into difficulties with their masters. Some slave-owners did not allow their darkeys to use tobacco, on account of the expense of providing it for them, and most of them loved it dearly. So these white people would give the darkeys tobacco for things which they would steal from their masters for them. It was often the case that a slick white family would get most of their living by having a slave or two to steal for them, and would pay the negro in tobacco, which he would use when his master was not around.

Sometimes a white person would have a grudge at a slave-owner, and hire or persuade a slave to do some damage to his master. A negro was generally so careless about doing a thing of this kind that his master would have no difficulty in tracing the crime to the one who did it. Then if this darkey's hide would not hold shucks for a few days, it was nobody's fault but his. Sometimes a slave would be persuaded or even hired to leave his master by some rascal who did not care how much beating the poor darkey got, but only how much trouble he could cause his owner.

Generally darkies were given from sundown Saturday until sunup Sunday, and some until sundown Sunday, but they were given to understand that when their furlough was out, they must be on hand. This was perfectly right, but there were many of them that would scarcely ever come in on time, and thus got themselves into trouble. When you come to think about the worry and trouble a dozen or more slaves would cause their owner, it is no wonder that many of them were punished. I do not see how they could ever have been controlled without it, and made to work enough to pay for their keeping.

The darkies were annoyed to a most unlimited extent by white persons who practiced tricks on them. They were passionately fond of 'possum and sweet potatoes. Nearly every family of darkies had one or more good hunting dogs, and the masters allowed them to go out hunting, as the animals were plenty, and gave much trouble about the raising of chickens. Of course, the potatoes could be had for the digging. These white men would slip out into the woods, covered with sheets, and scare the darkies almost to death. As soon as they saw the "haunt," they would break through the woods in a run, often losing axe, 'possums, and sometimes a sack of potatoes found (?) on the way. This was fun for the white men, but hard on the darkey's nerves. He might get over his scare in a few days by finding out that some white man had played a trick on him, but the loss of that 'possum and that bunch of potatoes would cause an "aching void" that would last for months. Sometimes when 'possum, and not fun, was the object, the poor fellows would be actually "held up" at the point of a gun, or a drawn club, and made to hand over their game. In some cases a darkey would show fight, and exercise his muscles in defending his game, and, in that case, usually carried it home.

Speaking of the punishing of slaves, reminds me of a funny incident that happened when I was a boy. My master, Mr. Jackson, had three other negro women who had children besides my mother. There was quite a crowd of us children when we were altogether. Master had a large cucumber patch, and one day we young ones decided to make a raid on the cucumbers, which we did. While we were busy gathering cucumbers, Master Jackson came along and called us all out into the road. We were all very badly scared, for we expected to get a good flogging. He placed us all in a row, facing the fence, with our bare feet in the dust, and then came around with a switch. He walked along and made a mark around each little negro's feet, so that he could see if he moved out of his tracks. I was the largest one, and had been placed head. When he was through marking around our feet, he stepped up to the fence, which was a common rail fence, and with his switch in one hand, he raised up about three of the top rails, and bad me march up and put my head into the crack. I, of course, had to do it, which I did as meekly as a lamb led up to a butcher's block. When my head was through, he began to let the rails down lightly on my neck, and I commenced screaming at the top of my voice, "Oh, Lord, massa, you is breaking my neck short off." I continued to beg and scream, and promise to be as good as an angel, if he would not kill me. He let down the rails just enough so that I could not jerk my head out, and began switching me where my body was bent and my dress the tightest. I soon saw that I could stand it all right, and it tickled me most to death to think that I would get to stand out in the road and watch a dozen little negroes go through the same performance. As soon as he had switched me a little he turned me loose and yelled out to me, "Back into your tracks, Pharaoh." I jumped back into my tracks, anxious to see the next boy's neck broken like mine was. But I had created such a scene over my affair that the others were so scared that they were having a regular buck-ague, and some of them had even staggered out of their tracks. To make it harder on them, if possible, I was holding my neck and making a hideous face, but most of it in an effort to keep from laughing aloud.

At last Master called to the next boy to come up and take his medicine. The boy was so scared that he could not move, and when Master called him again, the poor fellow managed to mutter out, "O, Lordy massa, would you kill a poor little nigger for a green cucumber?"

Master was so tickled that he did not call any more up to the fence, but just passed along and gave each of them a lick or two with the switch.

But the masters or their overseers were the only persons who were allowed to whip a slave, and no master would permit any one else to strike one, or mistreat him, unless the slave was acting very badly.

I remember at Clarksville, some mechanics were working across the river at Klipper's landing, building some houses: and the overseer on our plantation had told the slaves that if any of the mechanics called across the river to get over, that whoever of them that was the nearest should take the canoe to him, and bring him across. One day, a mechanic by the name of Wilkinson called over for a negro boy to bring the canoe to set him across. The boy took the canoe, and the man got into the vessel and stood up while the boy paddled it across. When the canoe struck the bank, the man pitched forward out into the mud and water, which he should have known would have happened to him. It was so funny that the boy laughed, which made Wilkinson so mad that he struck the boy a hard blow or two on the head. The boy's father was working near by, and the boy went and told him all about it. The boy's father called to the mechanic, and told him that he would give him his choice to take a whipping from him, then and there, or he would go and report him to the overseer. The man argued with the old negro a while, but it was no use, and he had to take his choice at once. So, after studying over it as long as the old negro would allow him to, he at last concluded to take a whipping from the old slave. The boy was sent for a good switch, and the old negro gave him a sound flogging, and that settled it.

It was a general weakness among slaves to steal, not that they always needed the things they took, but with some it seemed an impossibility to resist the temptation; but I know from a long experience that the negroes did not steal everything that was missed. There were thieves among the whites, and they generally managed to get out of being accused by charging it to the negroes on general principles. Personally, my greatest temptations were sweet potatoes in 'possum time, and the darkey's most delicious fruit, the watermelon. A watermelon patch was never any safer in Virginia or Tennessee, than an African cane patch from a drove of monkeys.

We had, on our plantation near Clarksville, large watermelon patches, but it was big fun to swim the river over to Klipper's, and then if any of our master's melons were missed, it could not be traced to us. With these advantages, and the melons as an inducement, I, with some other boys, would make regular voyages across the Roanoke and Dan, when the sun was not shining; and paddle over two large melons apiece. The way we would manage the melons was to break off the stems rather long, tie a string to each of them, and swing them around our necks. When once in the water, they would float, and not be any weight much upon our necks in swimming.

But I made some dangerous trips and came near being drowned several times. A great deal of chicken stealing was very justly charged to the darkeys, especially when there was to be a big negro frolic. A negro knew just how to take a chicken from a tall roost without noise. On a cold night, he would heat a piece of plank and hold it up in front of a chicken, and it was said that they would step off the limb right on to the warm plank, and could be carried any distance.

The darkey's jolly nature responded perfectly to any kind of excitement that produced pleasure, or was connected with any kind of fun. In the earlier days of slavery, musical instruments were too expensive to be owned by the average negro; but he managed to remedy this condition by making a gourd fiddle. This he would string up with catgut strings, likewise of his own make, and it was astonishing how much music they could get out of this funny looking instrument. A banjo was not very hard to make. Almost any common mechanical genius could take an ordinary meal sieve hoop, fit a neck to it, stretch a raw cathide across it, put on some catgut strings, and a banjo would be made that almost any darkey could beat enough music out of to keep up an uproar all night at a darkey dance. The white man is just as skillful with his fingers in making the notes; he learns the tune perfectly, and can sing it through; he can execute perfectly the steps in all the leading jigs, but there is something entirely original and peculiar in the negro's use of his fingers on the banjo; of his voice and action in singing; and his carriage in the dance; and something that the white man may imitate more or less closely, but he can never duplicate the old-time darkey and his banjo.

Speaking of the negro and the banjo reminds me of a circumstance that was told to me when I was a young man, and was said to be true. There was to be a wedding of two darkeys, a big potato and 'possum feast, and, of course pumpkin pie, and such other dainties as delight a darkey's soul, and all of it to be wound up with a big negro frolic. All the darkies from all the surrounding neighborhoods were invited, and had been for a week, the most faithful, industrious beings that ever lived in order to merit and earn the privilege of getting off early Saturday evening in order to attend the big affair. At that time, the country was thinly settled, and the houses were scattered about in patches of clearing, with large forests of timber between them. By the time the darkeys got their feeding done, and supper eaten, it was dark, and there were plenty of wild animals that frequently disputed a darkey's right to travel a certain path after night, and the darkey would always be obliging enough to seek safety in rapid flight, and allow the bear or wolf or whatever it might happen to be, an undisputed right of way.

It happened that one darkey, living in a remote neighborhood, was selected to be the chief one at the ceremony, and afterward, was to be accorded the honored privilege of making the music, and calling off the figures in the dance that was to last far into the Sabbath day. This darkey had been at great pains stringing up his banjo in the most substantial manner, and made every possible preparation for discharging the duties assigned him. It so happened, however, that he was rather late in getting a start for the scene of the fun and festivity, but undaunted, and without a single misgiving as to his ultimate success in reaching there in time, he started on his way, banjo in hand. The way was through a mile or so of thick forest, with only a narrow, unfrequented road through it, and only one cabin on the way, in a patch of cleared ground, which he knew to be unoccupied.

But calling up all the courage possible, and possessing a realizing sense of his own special importance on the present occasion, he boldly struck out at a rapid pace, along the dark, solitary way. It was so dark that the only way he could tell about the road was by watching for the opening of the timber overhead. He was frequently startled by the hoot of an owl, but this did not affect him much except to increase his feeling of loneliness. He had proceeded about half way through the woods to the deserted cabin when his blood was almost chilled at the sound of the howl of a wolf directly behind him, and not very far away. This was followed by seemingly a dozen more in rapid succession. He was now quite sure that he was being closely pursued by a full pack of hungry wolves, and he knew that his only chance to save himself was to run with all his might to the empty cabin, and hoped, if he could to reach it in time to fasten the door and keep out the wolves until some one would find out his condition and rescue him. So, he broke into a mad run for the clearing, but the road was so rough, and the night was so dark, that he found it exceedingly difficult to maintain what he considered a sufficient speed to outstrip his hungry pursuers. Several times he stumbled headlong over a stump, and it is a wonder that he did not break his banjo. Once, he lost his hat, but did not stop to get it. It perhaps saved his life; for when the wolves came to where it was, they stopped long enough to tear it to pieces, and to satisfy themselves that that was all that was left. Then mad and howling with hunger and rage, they sprang forward on the trail, but the delay had enabled the poor negro to run several yards, and to lessen the distance to the cabin to that extent. At last, as the savage brutes were drawing near to their intended victim, a cleared spot of ground and a lonely cabin a short distance ahead greeted the eyes of the frightened darkey who was running as he had never run before, and scared as he had never been before. But the alarming truth flashed across his mind that the wolves were nearer to him than he was to the cabin, and realizing this fact came near paralyzing him, but calling together all his strength for another desperate effort, he plunged forward at the very top of his speed. Just as he reached the edge of the clearing the wolves were not a dozen yards behind. He could now distinctly hear the sound of their approaching footsteps, and the snapping of their sharp teeth. For some reason, he decided to change his banjo to his left side, leaving his right arm free, when he accidently drew his trembling fingers across the strings, making a very loud noise.

This noise seemed to have some magical effect on the brutes, which ceased their howlings, and apparently almost stopped. But only for a moment; then with renewed howlings they again dashed forward, and would have been up with him ere he reached the cabin, when he again with considerable force, drew his fingers rapidly across the strings of his banjo, which had the effect to again check them long enough for him to spring into the cabin, and slam the door shut. He then barricaded the door with a heavy puncheon, which kept them out until he had time to regain his breath, and decide upon some mode of action, as he felt certain that they would very soon effect an entrance into the cabin. The old roof had fallen in, and the long, bare weight-poles were just above his head. Taking his banjo in one hand, and with a jump he caught one of the poles with the other hand, and swung himself up astride the ridge pole, but not a minute too soon, as several ugly noses were already prying open the door, and by the time he was seated, the combined weight of half a dozen of the ferocious creatures caused the puncheon to give way, and the door swung open. In rushed the whole pack, eager to make a quick supper on the negro, whom they supposed must be just on the inside.

Round and round they went, searching every nook and corner, when at last one of them spied him on the pole above. With a mighty spring and a powerful snap of its great jaws, it came near reaching a foot that was dangling rather low. Immediately a general assult by means of powerful jumps was made on the darkey's position, each jump being accompanied by

88

a clash of teeth that could be heard fifty yards away. These assaults were all directed at the part of the darkey that hung the lowest down, and pieces of his already tattered garments were frequently caught and torn off by the savage brutes. He could fancy to himself that they were becoming more desperate and intent upon reaching him, and he shifted his position so as to put every part of him likely to be reached by them out of the way. In doing so, he again disturbed the strings on his banjo, and again the beasts quieted at the sound. Then a happy thought came into his mind. He might save himself by playing tunes on his banjo. He thought he would try just the mere noise at first, and if that succeeded he would put his banjo in tune and give them some of his best performances, as they seemed to be doing their best for him. Again, as before, the sound produced by the banjo seemed to bewilder them, and they seemed to be half inclined to flee, but goaded by hunger, they would renew their frantic efforts to reach him. Then, the darkey, more hastily than ever before in his life, put his banjo in tune for an Old Virginia breakdown, and began clawing off the music in a furious way, when the wolves would subside, and most of them slink out to the outside, and scratch at the walls of the old cabin. But when the negro became tired, or stopped to tune his banjo for something else, they would immediately rush in, and seem determined, more than ever, to reach him. Again he would strike up some old familiar plantation melody, during the performance of which, the savage brutes would be more quiet. So, realizing that his safety depended upon his ability to pour into the ears of these beastly denizens of the forest, a steady stream of music, he applied himself, with all possible industry to the execution of all the reels, jigs, and ho-downs that he ever knew or heard. He kept this up without a minute's intermission until nearly daylight, when the darkeys at the frolic, which was only about a half mile away, hearing the continual howling of the wolves at the cabin, and suspecting that they had besieged some one in it, came with dogs and guns, run the savage brutes away, and rescued the frightened, and much exhausted darkey.

It is needless to say that his non-appearance at the big frolic was a great disappointment, perhaps felt more keenly by himself than by any one else. And if that darkey did not turn white, or his hair straighten out, it was not because he was not scared badly enough.

The great advantage of the slave to the family of the owner during the civil war can not be over estimated. Thousans of families depended almost entirely during times of peace upon the labor of the slave. When the war came up, nearly all the slave owners were on the side of the Confederacy, against the Federal government, and most of them went into the service, either as officers or as soldiers. This left the slaves as the sole dependence of the family, to take care of the stock and property; to guard and protect the family, and to cultivate the farms in order to produce a living. With the Confederates, it was different from the Federals. General Grant said the South had to "rob both the cradle and the grave" for soldiers. This meant that even the boys and the old men were compelled to go into the army. While at the North only the able-bodied men of middle age were required to go into the service. This left at home the young men and the older men to carry on the work and the business. But in the South there were none left who could work but the darkeys. The people at the North foresaw that if the war continued long that all of the male population would be pressed into the service, and many of them were tickled at the idea that the darkeys would not work without masters to drive them; that the farms and property would go to destruction through neglect; and that the families of the Southern men would starve when their living depended upon the darkeys. But how badly they were mistaken, the world now knows. With but few exceptions these slaves went about their work with greater diligence, and were more careful and industrious owing to the greater responsibilities placed upon them in their master's absence. True enough, many of the wives, and sometimes a daughter, would assume the duty of overseer and direct the farming affairs, but after all, the judgment of the darkey, in executing the work was the secret of success. He cultivated and gathered unmolested, the crops, when the owner would have run a great risk of his life even to be seen in the community. When the "enemy," as the Federals were called, were known to be coming through the community, the colored man well knew how little sympathy and respect they had for all things belonging to the rebels, that they secreted everything capable of being hidden from the Yankees, and thus saved it for the family. The corn and bacon were carried to caves, or cellars were dug in the side of the hill, the produce put in, and covered over with dirt and leaves until all danger had passed. The horses and cattle were haltered and driven off into some far-off thicket, and allowed to remain until the soldiers had passed on. Pens were built off in the woods and the hogs coaxed into them, to remain until the Yankees were gone.

If thieves or prowlers came around, day or night, the darkey knew how to use a musket, and would not hesitate to do so in order to protect "missus" and the children.

During the war, two Yankees came to the home of Mr. Octavius Yoe, who lived six miles above Rutledge. It was dark when they came, and chickens seemed to be the sole object of their mission. One of them took a light and climbed up into the hen house, and would hand down the chickens to the other man at the door, who would wring off their heads, and pitch them out into the yard. They would flutter out into the darkness, where a daughter of Mr. Yoe and several small negro children were standing. One of these would pick up the chicken, hand it to another, this one would pass it to another and so on until one of them would carry it off and hide it. This continued until every chicken had been taken from the roost and killed. Then the Yankees started to gather up their chickens and leave, but lo! and behold! not a chicken could be found. Every one had disappeared. Then the wrath and rage of the soldiers knew no bounds. They cursed and swore and ripped and tore, and threatened all kinds of vengeance against the children unless the chickens were produced. But old "Aunt Lucy," the colored woman, and mother of some of the children, put on a bold and defiant front, and told them that she would break their heads if they dared to molest the children. After the departure of the soldiers, there was a general cleaning of chickens, which were dressed and packed away for home use.

But there was one thing that the darkies could not well hide, and that was the fence rails. If there was one kind of fire which a soldier enjoyed more than another it was one built of fence rails. I remember once on a cold November evening, a company of soldiers in passing through our community, stopped and pitched their camp for the night near the home of one of our neighbors. We all knew what this meant to the community, for, upon such occasions, everything in the shape of something to eat would most surely be in pressing demand. So, there was a general scramble to get out of sight everything possible; but if a soldier did not happen to see just what he wanted, he most always possessed the happy faculty of rightly suspecting about where it would likely be hidden, and could usually discover its whereabouts. But on this particular occasion, they seemed to have supplied themselves with necessary provisions, and proceeded at once to make fires. The soldiers, as you know, divide up into a certain number of squads called "messes," and each mess makes a fire for cooking and warming. The master of this farm was a soldier in the Confederate service, which, perhaps, the Yankees knew. The mistress was out watching, and heard the usual command given to "Fall a rail, and take the lap." She saw the command promptly obeyed by at least a half-a-hundred rails being lifted from as many panels. She thought she saw unmistakable signs of her fence being all burned up, and sent her old colored man over to the tent of one who appeared to be an officer, to beg him to not allow her fence to be all burned up. His temper seemed to have already been ruffled at something, and he replied somewhat sharply: "You just go back and tell that old stingy mistress of yours that we are just going to take off the top rail." So, it was observed that at each trip they always lifted off the top rail, but by the time camp was broken next morning, a goose could have stepped over that fence. The officer, of course, gave her a voucher for the property used, which, if she had taken care of, would have been paid in full. But most people considered these papers as no good, and destroyed them. Afterward they wished they had kept them.

It was often a most pitiful spectacle to watch the tired, hungry and thirsty soldiers march along. Many of them appeared to be lame, and many seemed to be sick. The Yankees generally had good shoes and clothes, as well as good tents, but the Confederates, especially toward the close of the war, presented a sad sight. They were very poorly clad, many of them had neither shoes nor blankets, and bore the marks of exposure, hunger and fatigue. All soldiers, of either side, learned that the slaves were friends of a needy soldier, and would render him every aid in their power. Many a poor, hungry soldier has in the dark hours of night crawled from his tent, crept as noiselessly as a cat by the sentinel on his beat, and made his way to the cabin of some old darkey, and there was given a supper of bacon, corn bread, and coffee, perhaps in quantity, in excess of a whole week's rations.

A company of Confederate soldiers was passing through a neighborhood that had been relieved of almost everything eatable, and their only subsistence was a short allowance of hard tack. They halted at noon at a spring of water for the double purpose of resting, and of washing down the hard tack with the spring water. About the time they were preparing to remount and resume their march, one of the soldiers was observed a short distance from the camp eating green persimmons. The officer, somewhat exasperated at the seeming indifference of the soldier to the command to remount, called out very sharply, and demanded to know why he was eating the green persimmons. The soldier promptly answered, "To draw up my stomach to fit my rations, sir."

Speaking of the war reminds me of several funny incidents. A soldier, when he was not wounded and in a hospital, or exposed in the firing line of a battle or skirmish, or amid the dead and dying on the battlefield, could be quite humorous, and get off many amusing sayings.

As you know, in the South, before the war, the large slave owners kept a large, fierce species of bloodhounds to hunt down the runaway negroes who would flee from their cruel masters and take refuge in the swamps. So many horrible stories had been told of darkies being run down and torn to pieces by these ferocious dogs, that it is said General Sherman gave orders to his soldiers to kill every one of these dogs that they saw. On one occasion while they were passing a farm house in Georgia, a small poodle dog, the idol and pet of the household, ran out, barking fiercely. A soldier immediately caught up the little dog, and went on carrying the little animal to a convenient place of execution. The lady of the house came out screaming for the soldier to turn loose her pet. The soldier answered that they had orders to kill every bloodhound they could find. "But that's no bloodhound," exclaimed the lady. "But, madam," replied the soldier, "there is no telling what he may grow up into if we leave him," and the poor dog was carried on to his death.

Equally amusing were some of the replies and remarks made to the people who would interpose an objection when a demand was made for any kind of supplies. Once, during Sherman's march to the sea, the army was passing near a farm house, and a soldier darted out of ranks, and ran around to the barn, evidently in quest of chicken. Here he was confronted by the lady of the house, who politely asked the soldier to leave her chickens alone. He seemed disposed to press his demand for a chicken. He was then told that this special flock of fowls had been spared by all the troops that had passed that way, and that the commanding general had issued a special order for the protection of these very fowls. The soldier listened attentively to all of these arguments, and then gravely remarked, "Madam, what you say, no doubt, is true, but this rebellion must be put down if it takes every chicken in the Confederacy to do it." And, so saying he appropriated one of the finest of them, wrung off its head, stuffed it into his knapsack, and hurried on to overtake the command.

Since the darkeys, on the big plantations, were most generally appealed to for victuals by the hungry soldiers who chanced to camp in the vicinity, they were treated by the troops with about as much consideration as were the whites, and they received many favors from them that would have been denied them by the white folks.

On one occasion, a soldier called to an old darkey's cabin to borrow a skillet to take to his camp a short distance away. The old woman was very particular to have all her cooking vessels as clean as could be. She agreed to lend the skillet to the soldier, and handed the vessel to him. Instead of taking it, and carrying it away, he began turning it over, and inspecting it very closely. The old woman thinking that he suspected it not to be clean, became somewhat angered, and told him that he need not be afraid the vessel was not clean. The soldier replied that the skillet was all right, but that he was just thinking how nice it would be if he had some meat to fry in it.

Whereupon, the old woman cut off a generous hunk of bacon, and handed it to the soldier, who went on to camp rejoicing.

SUPERSTITION.

Well, yes, I suppose the negroes, on the whole, have more superstitution about their beliefs than the average white people have. I think I can easily account for this. In the first place, the negro race have not had the same advantages of education as the white people, even if they had as good minds, which some deny, and are therefore ignorant; and where you see an ignorant person, you will see one who can be made to believe almost anything. In the next place, the negroes have been always taught to believe in strange things, and such beliefs are slow to die out, when the white people were making an effort to keep it up. Some would tell them all kinds of terrible things just for fun, while others would use this method of getting them to do things that they would not otherwise do. Many a poor negro has been taken advantage of in this way, and a slave made of his mind as well as of his body. No doubt they were often scared into being religious, with the hope that they would be more honest and faithful.

But, I tell you, things have happened that tried the souls of more people than the negroes. The earthquakes of 1811 and 1812, were looked upon by both white and black, as the forerunner of some great calamity such as war, or the day of judgment, and it didn't matter which to us, as one was to be dreaded about as much as the other. It, however, made some difference among the people, for the good, religious people would say they would rather the judgment day would come, as they were ready to change their home-spun rags for ascension robes, but many of us said that if it were left to our choice, we would take our chances in war. The shocks were felt for a distance of over 300 miles, and the people were wild with fear and excitement. Many left their business and their work and made a rush for the church houses, believing that God would not allow them to be destroyed, and also, some to engage in prayer in order to complete their preparation for another world; and still others, who felt that they had already "made their peace-calling and election sure," to enter into a thanksgiving that the Great Day had at last come. Some were so overcome with feat of the dread calamity that they could not move, and I have heard of some who were actually frightened to death. But the earthquakes were not all. Just about the time the preachers who had assured the people of the certain coming of the day of doom, were explaining why it had not taken place, the great comet of the same year, came streaming across the sky! Oh, that was a sight never to be forgotten while one lives who saw it. It was of great size, and lighted the earth as bright as day. This wonderful comet coming as it did almost at the same time as the earthquakes, was a circumstance so powerful as to alarm the stout-hearted ones who laughed before, and when the great northern light which reddened the northern sky like a rising sun for months, happened at about the same time, the people all came to the conclusion that something dreadful was going to take place, and that the Lord was giving the people warning so that they might not be taken unawares. I shall never forget these times, how, after the day's work, the darkeys would gather in the log cabins, and pray, and sing soul-stirring songs until they were so exhausted that they fell asleep. The preachers, on Sunday, would create a panic in the church by their references to these events, and the excitement would continue during the week, with the people at their homes. If a person did not believe in something terrible going to happen, he did not speak out his mind.

Soon after this, as you know, the War of 1812 came on with its bloodshed and destruction of property; and following this, the massacres of white people by the Indians. Many, in fact, about all the people, accepted these wars as an explanation for these awful signs. But the most trying time on the souls of poor, ignorant mortals that I ever saw was when the great shower of falling stars took place in the year 1833. At night the heavens resembled a snow storm, with the flakes falling. The wildest excitement prevailed among all classes of people. Everywhere the people gathered there was singing, praying, and shouting. It was an evidence and a sign so powerful and convincing that many people went to their enemies to whom they had not spoken for years, each acknowledging his faults to the other, and making friends so that the Judgment day would find their hearts right. Some acted in a funny way, others, it was pitiful to see their actions. Some became so nervous that they never got over it while they lived. Very few people expected to see the world stand for any length of time, and they simply let all home and business affairs go.

THE UNDERGROUND RAILROAD.

There has always been a large class of people who have maintained against all arguments that human slavery is an unmixed evil; that all men are created, and remain in the sight of their Creator equal; that all apparent social and intellectual differences is due, not to any inherent superiority of the one nor the inferiority of the other, but to a difference in environment or condition; and that equal advantages of culture and refinement, would place them on an equal plane. While, on the other hand, a great number of people defend the institution from various standpoints, as right. It is highly probable that but few of any of the arguments, pro or con, was entirely without prejudice, which was sure to outcrop in the controversies and lend coloring and feeling to the discussions. It was noticeable, however during the heated word encounters, that the strongest defenses in the way of arguments generally proceeded from those persons who owned several slaves, or was directly benefited by their labor. True enough, sometimes, you would hear of some poverty-stricken person who never owned an acre of land, much less a negro, speak of "fighting for our negroes." The sentiment against the slavery of the African race was kindled to a very high pitch several years before the breaking out of the civil war. Many of the most influential papers, the most eloquent preachers, and the very ablest statesmen of the country engaged in an unrelenting war on slavery, and many good people devoted their lives and their fortunes toward the abolition of slavery. Many of them accomplished a great deal in the way of moulding public opinion, while the zeal of many "was not according to knowledge," and they actually injured the cause by attempting too much, or by pursuing the wrong methods to accomplish their ends. Many a poor misguided man like poor old John Brown whose zeal for a noble cause took on the form of fanaticism, was a victim to an ill-timed movement, that seemingly a sober thought would convince him that it could but result in failure and disaster. The cause of abolition suffered more from such abortive steps than from the combined arguments of the pro-slavery men.

One reason why the North wanted slavery abolished was that slave labor had ceased to be profitable in that manufacturing section. There was a demand for the skilled labor of the mechanic or the artisan, but not the crude labor of the negro. Perhaps, also, a certain feeling of jealousy at the rapidly increasing prosperity and development of the South, under slave labor, had something to do with the ardor of their arguments. It was true that the labor of the slave in the cotton and cane fields of the South was becoming more and more profitable, and more and more in demand as the invention of machinery caused an increased use of cotton, and as the markets of the world were opened for the sale of sugar.

But the efforts of those fighting the institution of slavery, and those interposing barriers in the way of its extension, were not confined to the North, but every possible method was employed to produce discontent in the minds of the slave. The prosperity and happiness of the negro in the free states of the North, with his little farm and home, with plenty of labor and good pay, with the freedom and liberty of his white neighbor-- this and much more--much of it without due regard always to truth--was told to the slave of the South, and no wonder it worked on his feelings even to the point of revolt or attempted escape. It was not necessary that the missionary of freedom should visit every plantation and present this picture to each slave, but communicate it to a few in each neighborhood, and it would spread from lip to lip, from plantation to plantation, like wild fire, until the brain of the entire negro population of the South was inflamed. Then it became only a question of courage or of daring as to who would make the effort to escape. To a majority of them it appeared a hopeless task to evade blood-hounds and cruel slave hunters in an effort to reach a Northern state, and here many decided to resign themselves to their fate and remain. Many who might undertake the venture were hampered with a wife and children which they could never think of leaving; but instances are on record where a man would be successful in reaching a free state and gain his freedom, and long afterward, "when the cruel war was over," be rejoined by his long-abandoned family, and spend the remainder of their days together. But there would usually be found a man on nearly every large plantation who would incur the risk of pursuit, capture, and perhaps death, and boldly set out for the "promised land," as the North was called. He usually had no difficulty in finding one or more individuals as desperate and daring as himself, and the perilous journey would begin. These fugitives had been assured that after they had escaped from their immediate neighborhood they would find white men who would conceal them from their pursuers, supply them with food, and when danger of capture was past, direct them on to other white persons, who would do the same for them, until they would be safely escorted to a land of liberty. Night time, of course, was selected in which to set out on the journey, and most, if not all their travels were by the light of the moon and stars. The line of persons who had thus secretly banded themselves together for the purpose of aiding slaves to escape to free territory was termed the Underground Railroad. They stretched across the country as a chain, from the far South to various points in the borders of free states. If only a slave could the first or second night succeed in finding one of these "agents" he would have a reasonably fair chance of ultimate success, but it was by no means certain that the combined efforts of the Underground Railroad operators could prevent his being overtaken and captured. Whenever the fugitive reached the home of one operator, if enough darkness remained, he was conveyed in some manner, to the home of the next one who would conceal him until night again came on, and then convey him to the next station. The roads were not generally used, but the way usually led across hills, ridges, and even mountains by unfrequented paths, and as pursuit in every case was to be expected, the greatest caution had to be exercised in order to throw off the bloodhounds from the track as often as possible by various methods. These vicious dogs were nearly always used to hunt down the slave, and the fierce bark of the blood-thirsty animal on his trail would be sufficient to send a thrill of despair through his frame. Often, however, he was provided with a gun and bayonet with which he would frequently succeed in killing or wounding the dogs, and finally escape. Some of the most thrilling incidents of encounters with these ferocious brutes are related by those who have been thus pursued and attacked by them. Often, without any means of defense against them, when overtaken, the poor man was obliged to climb out of their reach and there patiently sit and wait for his pursuers to come up, who would make him come down and, handcuffed, drive him back again to a more galling bondage. But many resolved on starting to escape or to die in the attempt, and would provide the necessary means of defense or protection, and many instances are on record of bloody encounters with such desperate fugitives, when overtaken by dogs or men. They would fight to the death, and would struggle with their pursuers with the madness of desperation, and often leave men and dogs dead or dying, and renew their mad flight for freedom. And when, at last, they had succeeded, amidst suffering, hunger, hardship, and mortal dread of capture, in reaching a place where they were free, it was seldom to find what had been pictured to them, and never fully realizing their hopes and expectations. No doubt many a poor, deluded slave, stinging with the remorse of disappointment, would have gladly exchanged his Northern freedom for the plentiful hog and hominy of the sunny South. He could, in his solitude, be heard to hum the old familiar plantation melody,

"I's gwine back to Dixie; No more I'se gwine to wander."

The slave-power had enacted very stringent laws relating to runaway slaves. These laws imposed heavy fines and other penalties on all persons aiding in any way, slaves in escaping from their masters. To give them food or shelter, to conceal them from pursuers, to give them directions for traveling, constituted grave violations of these laws, and the offenders were prosecuted to their fullest extent. In very many instances, such heavy fines were imposed as to sweep away every dollar's worth of the violator's property.

Some who assisted slaves to escape to freedom were put into prison on the charge of slave-stealing, and there wore away, in dark, dingy, filthy cells, the best years of their lives, but without a murmur, as they had, at first, deliberately assumed the responsibility and consequences of such proceedings.

But the operators of this Underground Railroad seldom asked the name of an escaping slave, and and not often consented to listen to their tale of woe, for it was always presumed to be the same in every case. Neither would they ever disclose to a fugitive their own names, and, hence, escaped detection unless the slaves were found hidden on their premises, or were apprehended while in the act of conveying him away. In the latter case, immediate arrest, a trial before a pro-slavery court, and a sentence to the full limit of the law was imposed. Some active agents for escaping slaves were the victims of assassination; still people all over the country paid no heed to the summary execution of the fugitive slave laws, and voluntarily undertook the work, subjecting themselves to the vengeance of the slave hunters who usually posed as officers of the law.

In the state of Georgia, there was a slave and his wife in whose bosoms burned an unconquerable desire to breathe the air of freedom. This desire at last became so strong as to assume the form of a resolve to make the attempt. So many who had taken passage on the Underground Railroad, had been dragged back into slavery and cruelly punished for their attempted escape, that these two feared to undertake it. They thought over and discussed many plans, but each would seem to contain a weak feature that promised to defeat their efforts and cause the enterprise to result in failure. Then, too, so many had attempted, and so many had succeeded, that the slave owners were exercising increased vigilance, and the plans that had once succeeded, would be sure to fail now.

So, at last, they decided on a plan of escape. The man was very black, but at the same time very shrewd, and of the most engaging manners and conversation. The wife was very fair, the Saxton blood predominating to such an extent as to almost exclude the black. They decided that she was to assume the roll of a young Southern planter, who for some reason or other, was traveling North with his slave. She was to assume all the haughty

103

demeanor of the white slave owner, and, owing to her excellent judgment and rare presence of mind under trying circumstances, was able to do so admirably. They had calculated the close scrutiny to which they would be subjected, the reward that would be offered for their detection and return and the possible and probable contingencies that would arise, and so the wife decided on certain disguises to wear. She was, throughout the journey, to be the victim of a terrible toothache, and to have her jaws wrapped and bandaged so as to conceal certain of her features that might occasion suspicion, and subject her to an unceremonious examination which might prove annoying and certainly fatal to the undertaking. She of course, was, on account of her affliction, excused from conversations, and the slave, being fully equal to every occasion, would answer all questions for his young master, and make all explanations. Anticipating occasions where it would be necessary to register at hotels, the young man had met with the misfortune of a serious accident to his right arm which he carried in a sling. They did not take an underground route, but traveled in the most open manner by whatever conveyance was most convenient, be it railway, steamboat, or stage-coach; and by so doing made the journey much sooner than if they had adopted any other plan. The young planter was very closely questioned on many occasions, and detection seemed imminent more than once, but the ready wit and shrewdness of the slave servant, and the success of the pretended ailments of the young planter saved them. They passed through all the large cities from Macon to Philadelphia. Arriving safely at the latter place, they were free from danger at present, and the young planter's toothache was relieved, and his diseased arm cured, but his (her) nervous system had undergone such a strain that she was prostrated for quite a while. After a time they went to Boston to live, and were contented, happy, and prosperous until the fugitive slave laws were passed, and then the slave hunters were after them at once. Their friends would not allow them to be taken back to bondage, but to avoid the annoyance, they were aided in going to Great Britain, where they remained until the Emancipation Proclamation made them men and women instead of property, when they came back to

America, and settled in Georgia and lived in peace and happiness.

PHARAOH'S AGE--BILL OF SALE

The writer regrets that the limits assigned to this volume forbid the insertion of many interesting incidents related by this remarkable old man, and many particulars concerning his eventful life. He deems it sufficient, in closing, to state that Pharaoh was purchased by Mr. Jackson, and originally cost $1,000; but on account of his age, when sold at the administrator's sale, only brought $421, or less than half his former value. Though represented in the following Bill of Sale as fifty years of age, he was undoubtedly sixty or more. The writer is informed by several gentlemen, whose ages now range from seventy-five to ninety-three years, that Uncle Ferry was an old man, too old to do a regular slave's work when purchased by Mr. Chesney in 1841. Allowing him to have been sixty when sold in 1841--which is a very reasonable supposition--his present age would be one hundred and twenty-one years!

Following is a verbatim copy of the Bill of Sale, rendered to Mr. Chesney, on the purchase of Uncle Ferry (Pharaoh). The original document is now in the possession of Mr. W. R. Kelley, administrator of the estate of his grandfather, John Chesney, deceased. Mr. Kelley was, for several years, receiver of Ferry for the allowance to the old man from the county. Through his kindness the writer is enabled to present this copy to his readers. He also acknowledges other favors extended by the same gentleman in the preparation of this volume.

BILL OF SALE.

"Know all men by these presents that I, Corbin Jackson, administrator of the estate of Johnathan Jackson, deceased, for the sum of $421 paid by John Chesney, the receipt where-of is hereby acknowledged, did sell to the said John Chesney a certain mulatto man, a slave for life, named Ferry, fifty years of age at the time of sale, which took place about November 25, 1841. I, the administrator of the said estate of the said Johnathan Jackson, did in November, 1841, sell the said Ferry a slave for life, and deliver him to the said John Chesney, his heirs and assigns forever. I do hereby warrant and forever defend the title to said slave, Ferry, to the said John Chesney, his heirs, etc., against the lawful claims of all manner of persons whatsoever. In witness whereof, I do hereunto subscribe my name and affix my seal. January 8, 1841. All of Grainger County, Tennessee.

(Signed) CORBIN JACKSON. (Seal).

Test: Sam Shields, Thomas Mynatt, William Sevier."

His X mark.

On the back is marked, "Corbin Jackson, Bill of Sale to John Chesney, Yellow Boy, Ferry."Remark--The name Pharaoh was shortened, for convenience in speaking it, to "Farry," which was corrupted to "Ferry," as the old man has always been called.

CONCLUSION.

"Mors propter brevitatem vitae nunquam longe abest."

Last of the pioneers! And soon, perhaps before these pages meet the eye of the reader, will the oar of the silent boatman touch the shore of time for this last one. Soon will thrill for the last time the time-worn frame, and rekindle the time-dimmed eye for the last time at the recital of incidents, and awakened memories of sights and scenes of long ago. And when these lips have embraced the silence of the grave, then will go down the curtain on the rich stores of tradition and reminiscence which will be forever lost to the world. The lights then extinguished will burn in no other hands, and the task of rescuing the already fading memories of those who will soon be no more, will perhaps be appreciated.

The sole representative of pioneer days sits calmly in his cabin awaiting the summons for his departure to a republic where the slave is at last equal with his master; where the creditor loses his usury, and the debtor is acquitted of his obligation; where comfort comes to all whom time can not console; and freedom to all whom time can not release.

Brevis a Deo nobis vita data est; at memoria bene redditae vitae sempiterna.

FINIS

In Memoriam
PROF. J. C.

In Memoriam
PROF. J. C. WEBSTER.

WEBSTER.

[Prof. J. C. Webster.]

The subject of this sketch, Prof. J. C. Webster, was not an ordinary man. He ideally combined his qualities of cheerfulness and serious mindedness, of work and the preparation for work.

Intellectually, he was endowed with a strong balanced mind, a firm will, and good executive powers. He was unusually fitted for his work; and this he did thoroughly. He was a teacher by vocation, by choice, and by due preparation. During vacations and leisure moments while teaching he accomplished many other things, being a surveyor of unusual ability, was editor of three newspapers at different times, and was author of a book called "The Last of the Pioneers." He served as County Superintendent of Public Instruction of Morgan County. During the recent war he rendered to his country an invaluable service, being connected with the work of the Red Cross, Food Administration and Council of National Defense.

In his earlier years, while pursuing his work at the University of Tennessee he taught classes in that institution. He was teacher in the Hampden Sidney school in Knoxville for a number of years and received repeated offers of the chair of mathematics at the University but did not accept, preferring to work in the rural districts and in this way aid in furthering the educational system.

He had started on his fortieth year of educational work when his sickness cut short the many plans he had made for the cause. His pupils everywhere testify to his many helpful ideas and advice. He was always ready to speak an encouraging word to the one striving for an education and was the cause of many realizing their ambition. He counted among his students some of the most important business men of the state.

Though he is no longer present to continue his work, his influence will ever be present as an inspiration to those who knew him.

www.ingramcontent.com/pod-product-compliance
Lightning Source LLC
Chambersburg PA
CBHW070933290526
45795CB00001B/501